Sunday Best Baking™

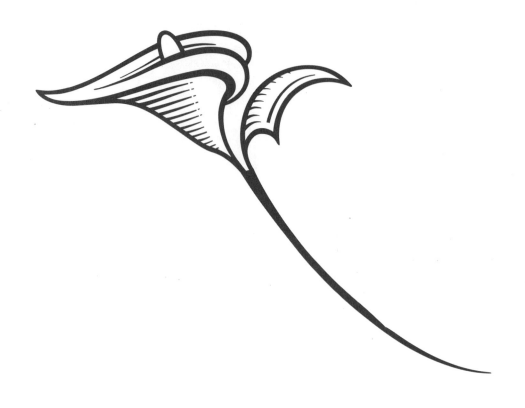

WHITE LILY®
A Southern Tradition Since 1883

Sunday Best Baking

Over a Century of Secrets
from the White Lily Kitchen

TM

LONGSTREET
Atlanta, Georgia

Published by LONGSTREET PRESS, INC.,
a subsidiary of Cox Newspapers,
a subsidiary of Cox Enterprises, Inc.
2140 Newmarket Parkway
Suite 122
Marietta, Georgia 30067

Printed in the United States of America

1st printing, 1998

Library of Congress Catalog Card Number: 98-066370

ISBN: 1-56352-529-1

White Lily is a federally registered trademark of The White Lily Foods Co., Knoxville, Tennessee.

"Flour Power," copyright © 1998 by Shirley O. Corriher

Compiled by Belinda Ellis Gibson
Text by Julie Maples
Photographs by Jerry Burns

A special thank you to Jeanne Voltz, a wonderful Southern cookbook author whose memories enliven these pages, and to Shirley O. Corriher, who graciously contributed an explanation of flours and her famous biscuit recipe.

Book and jacket design by Burtch Bennett Hunter

Contents

Introduction

Wonderful smells of fried chicken and fresh-baked bread float from the kitchen through the wide hallway and out onto the front porch. A slatted-back porch swing sways softly in the breeze.

It's Sunday. Church is over, and Grandmother is waiting.

Suddenly, car doors slam, the screen door creaks, footsteps clatter on the wooden floor, and voices fill the foyer. As the last pan of biscuits is pulled from the oven, tomatoes are sliced, and trays are filled with pickled peaches and watermelon, cousins spill into the entranceway to greet one another with hugs and jokes. Dressed in their Sunday best, the family gathers from miles around to continue a time-honored tradition – Sunday dinner.

The delicious aromas draw everyone into the dining room. The crowd nestles around the table, admiring the cream-colored linen cloth overlaid with lace, the rarely seen "fine" china, polished silverware, and glasses already filled with sweet iced tea.

But the crowning glory is the food. Platter after platter of wonderful, Southern-style meats, breads, and vegetables gently bump against the plates. As they say down here, Grandmother "sure sets a nice table."

There are mouthwatering stacks of fried chicken and ham, flaky biscuits and spoon bread, crisp-fried okra, mashed potatoes, purple hull peas and string beans, juicy stewed tomatoes with cornmeal dumplings, hot buttered corn, and Grandmother's creamy gravy.

As far as diets go, we will think about that tomorrow! Front and center on the oak sideboard, a towering red velvet cake with cream cheese icing beckons. A fresh peach cobbler, a rich pecan pie, and a double-crust apple pie await a topping of the homemade ice cream packed down in rock-salted ice.

With a prayer of thanksgiving, Sunday dinner is officially under way.

White Lily Flour is Sunday Best

Whether it was bought in barrels, sacks, or bags, White Lily flour has been a part of Southern culture and cuisine for 115 years. Many of us have childhood memories of watching the soft, floury hands of "Nanny" or "Mamaw" prepare food for the family. You can even still find folks who remember the clothes their mamas made from used-up White Lily flour sacks.

White Lily flour was called Sunday Best Flour because it was the best flour in the house. Just as people saved their finest clothes for Sunday, they also saved their finest flour to make the main meal of the week.

The Story of White Lily

Times past may have been slower and seemed simpler, but they certainly weren't easier. Around the turn of the century, cooks were baking on open hearths or wood-burning stoves. Quality baking flour simply wasn't available. Farmers would take their wheat and have it coarsely ground at gristmills, also called custom mills. The miller would take part of the ground flour as payment, and townspeople would buy the extra flour the millers collected.

J. Allen Smith, Founder of White Lily Foods in 1883

On July 16, 1883, Southerners' baking fortunes took a significant turn for the better. A visionary young businessman by the name of J. Allen Smith began grinding out barrels and barrels of flour in Knoxville, Tennessee, to be sold throughout the South. Obsessed with quality, Smith could not be content with mere quantity. He commanded the mill foreman to keep trying different milling methods to produce the best flour possible.

About a year later, the mill finally produced the flour Smith had been looking for. Rumor has it that one steamy morning in July the mill foreman walked into Smith's office and placed a small pouch of flour on the desk. "Mr. Smith," he said proudly, "you've been wanting a flour that's whiter than snow

2

The White Lily Mill in circa 1930, with its rooftop sign proclaiming "Friends Everywhere."

and smoother than silk. Well," he said, taking a pinch of flour and sprinkling it into J. Allen's palm, "I think you've finally got it."

Although most national flour brands are made from hard winter or spring wheat or from a blend of soft and hard wheat, both White Lily Plain All-Purpose Flour and Self-Rising Flour are made solely from soft, red winter wheat. This variety of wheat results in lighter, fluffier, and more tender cakes, pie crusts, and pastries as well as biscuits.

Cooks can shortcut most recipes by using self-rising flour instead of all-purpose. But for any recipe, you can substitute 1 cup of all-purpose flour plus 1½ teaspoons baking powder and ½ teaspoon salt for 1 cup of self-rising.

At White Lily, the wheat goes through a special milling process, then only the best 50 percent of the flour, called Fancy Patent Flour, is actually packaged and sold to home cooks. The rest is sold to commercial bakeries. The milling process creates a flour with lighter volume. In

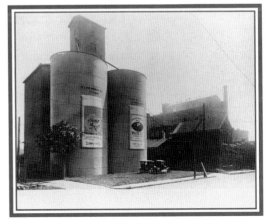

White Lily Mill Silos, circa 1920

fact, 1 cup plus 2 tablespoons of White Lily flour is equivalent to 1 cup of other brands. The high quality also means a brighter, whiter flour. You won't see the grayish-white color or the dark specs found in other flours.

The origins of the wheat and the care that goes into the milling are what make White Lily so much better for baking biscuits, breads, muffins, pie crusts, cakes, and all the other delights cherished by Southerners. Some of the finest Southern chefs will testify to advice given by their mothers before they set out on their own: "Don't ever bake with anything but White Lily."

Great Western Free-Swinging Sifter
Each box contains up to twenty-seven sifter screens made of silk or fine nylon.

And one Southern woman whose mother baked biscuits every night for supper even remembers her dad admonishing, "Don't be silly. Eat White Lily" when the kids weren't cleaning their plates.

So whether you're a seasoned veteran or a new cook to the kitchen, White Lily and *Sunday Best Baking*™ can help you give those you love your best, too. And that's one Southern tradition that's not likely to change.

Even famous stars living hectic Hollywood lives can't do without their White Lily flour. After Ned Beatty's mother and Jill St. John wrote to White Lily lamenting the lack of the company's products in California, White Lily decided to set up a special system to get their flour and cornmeal to people living outside the South.

You can now order White Lily through the mail by writing to them at White Lily Foods, P.O. Box 871, Knoxville, TN 37907. You can also order through their Web address, www.whitelily.com, or by calling 423-546-5511.

It's now no longer necessary for anyone, wherever they may be, to do without the luxury of White Lily.

Flour Power

By Food Scientist Shirley Corriher

Using the right flour for the job can mean the difference between success or failure of a dish, or at least the difference between a dish's being just OK or fabulously good. How is one flour different from another? How can a cook know which flour to use?

When the cook adds water to flour and stirs, two proteins in the flour, glutenin and gliadin, grab the water and each other to form springy, elastic sheets of gluten. If a flour has a lot of these proteins, it will absorb more water and make more gluten.

Different flours have different amounts of the two gluten-forming proteins. In general, soft winter wheats, grown in moderate climates where the ground never freezes to a depth greater than 10 inches, have less glutenin and gliadin. These lower protein flours are ideal for cakes, muffins, and pastry. Hard spring wheats grown in colder climates are usually higher in protein and make high-protein flour, outstanding for yeast breads.

Not only are there different strains of wheat, but flour from the same strain of wheat can vary. Many things – soil, temperature, rainfall, maturity at harvest – influence protein content. The milling process is also a major determinant of the protein content of flour. When flour is milled, wheat kernels are cleaned and tempered (soaked in water), then crushed and the germ and bran removed. The endosperm (main central portion of the kernel) goes through one set of rollers and sifters after another, and these grind, sift, and separate flour into fractions called *streams*. There may be more than eighty streams in this separation process. Just as wine makers blend juices from different vineyards to make fine wines, millers blend flour from different streams to make fine flours for different purposes.

Millers Custom-Blend "All-Purpose"

All-purpose flour can have as little as eight grams of protein per cup to more than thirteen grams per cup. The customers of millers in Southern states specialize in biscuits, cakes, and pie crusts and are accustomed to lower-protein flour (eight to nine grams per cup). So Southern millers blend fine low-protein flours from soft winter wheat. Millers in Northern states, which have an abundance of high-protein flour, blend their all-purpose – particularly their unbleached all-purpose – so that it's high in protein (thirteen grams per cup) for their customers. Northerners have made fine yeast breads with these flours for many years.

Lower Protein Flour: Less Gluten

Low-protein flours like White Lily's all-purpose and self-rising flours are ideal for anything that needs to be tender, like pie crusts, cakes, biscuits, muffins and quick breads, pancakes, and sauces and gravy. Most of these products are *chemically leavened* with baking powder and baking soda. Baking powder and soda work in an entirely different way than yeast. If you add hot water to baking powder you will instantly see a great rush of fine bubbles. Strong sheets of gluten in high-protein flours actually interfere with this type of leavening by holding the mass of bubbles down.

Low-protein flours have long been prized in Asia for making soft noodles. Low-protein flour is also similar to Italian flour, and some Italian chefs love it (plain or mixed with a little semolina) for pasta.

Higher Protein Flour: More Gluten

The gluten in high-protein flours like White Lily's bread flour is ideal for yeast breads. Yeast oozes out a liquid that releases carbon dioxide gas and alcohol to inflate tiny bubbles already in the dough. The elastic gluten sheets expand during this steady, gentle inflating process, and the dough rises.

The elastic sheets of gluten are strong, tough, and hold things together. If the cookies are crumbly, you need more gluten. If the tops come off the muffins, you need more gluten. You want strong gluten for pizza, some pastas, and strudel dough that must be stretched thin and for puffed pastry, Danish, and croissants that must hold steam and puff apart.

Cooking teacher, food consultant, and award-winning cookbook author Shirley Corriher has been lecturing and writing about food for more than 20 years. She has made presentations to the Smithsonian Institution, the American Association for the Advancement of Science, the International Association of Culinary Professionals, and, in Europe, at two International Symposiums on Gastronomy and Science. She lives in Atlanta. She graciously allowed us to include her famous "Touch of Grace" biscuit recipe in Sunday Best Baking™.

Biscuits

If you want to hear Southerners indulge in sentimental nostalgia, just get them to describe their mamas' biscuits. A plateful of tender, hot, and flaky biscuits have been the ultimate breakfast in the South since fine-textured, soft-wheat flour and baking soda became available.

In fact, for a long time, biscuits were the only fast food in the South. Fast to make and easy to carry, a couple of them carried in a poke sustained you through long days in the fields, the mills, or wherever your work took you. And they provided the perfect afternoon pick-me-up for schoolchildren.

It was the commercial development of baking powder and baking soda, as well as the availability of affordable flour from commercial mills, that gave rise to the South's reputation for light and tender biscuits. When J. Allen Smith reopened the Knoxville Mills in Tennessee in 1883, bakers were quick to realize that what would come to be known as White Lily flour was perfect for making biscuits.

For many years, cooks whipped up batch after batch of biscuits for breakfast and dinner in their hand-hewn wooden bread bowls. First, the biscuit maker dipped a heaping teacupful of flour from the barrel to the shallow, long, hollowed-out piece of a small tree trunk called a dough bowl. She swept a pile of flour to one end of the bowl, then picked up salt, baking soda, and baking powder with her fingertips, gauging them by feel for amounts, and mixed them one by one into the flour. She worked in the shortening, tips of fingers flying through the dry ingredients as she rubbed it into flaky particles. Then she poured in cold buttermilk a bit at a time (most families owned a milk cow or patronized a neighbor who sold milk and butter stored in the springhouse). She kneaded the mixture together, rolled it out on a table sprinkled lightly with flour, cut it, and quickly placed the biscuits into a wood-fired, cast-iron cooking stove.

Nowadays, homemade biscuits are more often a weekend treat than an everyday occurrence. Although some of the mystique of making biscuits may have gone the way of the biscuit bowl, biscuits made any way at all are still as soul-satisfying as they always were. Be warned! Once you have made these a few times, you'll never be able to fake out your family with canned biscuits again.

THE SECRET TO SPEEDY BISCUITS

If a recipe calls for self-rising flour, but you have plain all-purpose flour on hand, use the simple formula below:

For one cup of White Lily Self-Rising Flour, substitute 1 cup of White Lily Plain All-Purpose Flour, 1½ teaspoons baking powder, and ½ teaspoon of salt.

FLOUR FINESSE

There are three kinds of wheat flour you can buy at the grocery store: flour made from soft winter wheat grown in the South and Midwest, flour from the hard wheat of colder climates, and flour that is a mix of both soft and hard wheat.

Soft wheat flour makes the soft, tender biscuits Southerners love. Hard wheat results in tough biscuits. Most national brand flours are a combination of hard and soft wheat. However, both White Lily Plain All-Purpose and White Lily Self-Rising Flour are 100 percent soft wheat flour.

White Lily "Light" Biscuits

The Southern custom of sopping biscuits in molasses or honey prevailed until recently. To sop, a half biscuit turned buttered side down in the molasses was pushed around with a fork to pick up sweetening. A bite was cut off with the fork and lifted to the mouth, without dripping on the breakfaster's shirt or the tablecloth. Sopping the biscuit with the hands was considered bad manners, and the child who did was admonished by his mother or father to "Use your fork!"

2 cups White Lily Self-Rising Flour
¼ cup shortening, butter, or lard
⅔ to ¾ cup milk or buttermilk

Preheat oven to 500° F.

Measure flour into a large bowl. Divide the shortening, butter, or lard into pieces and scatter on top of the flour. Work the pieces into the flour with a pastry cutter, two knives, or your fingertips until the pieces are about the size of peas. Gradually stir in milk or buttermilk, adding only enough to moisten the flour and hold the dough together.

Turn the dough onto a lightly floured surface. Knead gently two to three strokes. Using a light touch, pat or roll dough to ½-inch thickness. Cut with a floured 2-inch biscuit cutter, leaving as little dough between cuts as possible. Gather the remaining dough and re-roll one time. Discard scraps remaining after second cutting.

Place biscuits on a baking sheet with sides touching for soft Southern-style biscuits. If you prefer biscuits with crisp sides like those served by most fast food chains, place biscuits close together but not touching.

Bake for 8 to 10 minutes, or until the tops are golden brown. Serve hot out of the oven.

Makes 12 biscuits.

Variation

White Lily "Light" Drop Biscuits: For time-crunched cooks, drop biscuits are perfect. They have the added bonus of a crisp, crunchy top. Follow the recipe for White Lily "Light" Biscuits, except use slightly more milk — ¾ to 1 cup. Then drop dough, using a heaping tablespoon, onto baking sheet. Bake as instructed above.

Angel Biscuits

Hostesses and caterers bake these biscuits for parties. They can be baked ahead of time and served at room temperature or reheated by placing on a baking sheet, covering with foil, and warming in a 400° F oven for about seven minutes.

Butter, melted

1 package active dry yeast

2 tablespoons warm water (105° F to 115° F)

5 cups White Lily Self-Rising Flour

¼ cup sugar

½ teaspoon baking soda

1 cup shortening

2 cups buttermilk

Grease baking pan with melted butter. Dissolve yeast in warm water. Set aside. In mixing bowl, combine flour, sugar, and baking soda.

With pastry cutter or fork, cut in shortening until mixture resembles coarse meal. Combine buttermilk and yeast water. Add liquids gradually to flour mixture, stirring with fork until flour is moistened.

Turn dough onto lightly floured surface and roll out ½-inch thick. Cut with 2-inch biscuit cutter, dipping cutter into flour between cuts. Press cutter straight down without twisting for straight-sided, evenly shaped biscuits. Place close together in prepared pan. Cover with damp cloth and let rise one hour (dough does not double in size).

Bake in preheated 400° F oven for 15 to 20 minutes or until browned. Brush tops with melted butter while hot.

Makes 30 to 40 biscuits.

Circa 1883

White Lily Biscuits

The White Lily original biscuit recipe has made a century of light biscuits. Our recipe hasn't changed much over the years, but the original version included sugar — a sweet touch worth trying. White Lily Self-Rising Flour didn't exist when this recipe was written.

2 cups White Lily Flour

1 teaspoon salt and sugar

¼ teaspoon soda

2 teaspoons baking powder

4 tablespoons shortening

Scant cup fresh buttermilk

Sift White Lily Flour, salt, sugar, soda, and baking powder into mixing bowl. Chop in the shortening with knife or spatula, add buttermilk to make a soft dough. Toss on floured board, roll to ½-inch thickness, cut as desired, place on greased baking sheet, cook 8 minutes in hot oven 500 degrees.

"Touch of Grace" Biscuits

Award-winning author and food scientist Shirley Corriher actually carries this famous biscuit recipe in her purse to hand to those who ask for it. These are incredibly light, moist biscuits—truly memorable! Shirley recommends the low-protein White Lily Flour for tender, moist biscuits. Her recipe secret is a very wet dough. It makes more steam in a hot oven and creates lighter biscuits. You can make a lower-fat version by using fat-free buttermilk for all the liquid and reducing the shortening to 2 tablespoons.

Nonstick cooking spray
1½ cups White Lily Self-Rising Flour
1 tablespoon sugar
¼ heaping teaspoon salt
3 tablespoons shortening
½ cup cream, whipping or heavy
¾ cup buttermilk
1 cup White Lily Plain All-Purpose Flour
2 tablespoons butter, melted

Preheat oven to 450° F. Arrange a shelf in the center or just below the center of the oven, and spray a small (6- to 8-inch) round cake pan with nonstick cooking spray.

Combine the White Lily Self-Rising Flour, sugar, and salt in a medium mixing bowl. With your fingers or a pastry cutter, work the shortening into the flour mixture until there are no shortening lumps larger than a big pea.

Stir in the cream first, then the buttermilk. The dough should look like cottage cheese.

Pour the cup of White Lily Plain All-Purpose Flour onto a plate or pie tin. With a medium (2-inch) ice cream scoop or spoon, scoop a biscuit-size lump of wet dough into the flour and sprinkle some flour over it to coat the outside. Flour your hands well. Pick up the biscuit and shape it into the general shape of a soft round. At the same time, shake off the excess flour. As you shape each biscuit, place it into the pan, pressing each one against the other so that they will rise up and not spread out. Continue shaping biscuits in this manner until you use all of the dough.

Bake in the center or just below the center of the oven until lightly browned, about 20 minutes. Brush the biscuits with melted butter. Cool for one or two minutes in the pan, then dump out and cut the biscuits apart.

"Butter 'em while they're hot!" Split the biscuits in half, butter, and eat immediately.

Makes about 10 biscuits.

Note: Do not use self-rising flour for shaping since the leavener is not dissolved and used. It will give a bitter taste to the outside of the biscuits.

Country Ham and Cheese Biscuits

Cheese and ham in the biscuit dough make a hearty breakfast or accompaniment to salads or soup.

2 cups White Lily Self-Rising Flour
¼ cup shortening
1 cup finely chopped cooked country ham
1 cup shredded Swiss cheese
8 ounces (1 cup) sour cream
¼ cup milk or buttermilk
2 tablespoons butter, melted

Preheat oven to 450° F.

Measure flour into a large bowl. Divide shortening into pieces and scatter on top of the flour. Work the pieces into the flour with a pastry cutter, two knives, or your fingertips until the pieces are about the size of peas.

Add ham, cheese, and sour cream. Gradually add the milk or buttermilk, stirring only enough to moisten the flour and hold the dough together.

Turn the dough onto a lightly floured surface. Knead gently two to three strokes. Using a light touch, pat or roll dough to ½-inch thickness. Cut with a floured 2-inch biscuit cutter, leaving as little dough between cuts as possible. Gather the remaining dough and re-roll one time. Discard scraps remaining after second cutting.

Place biscuits on a baking sheet with sides touching for soft Southern-style biscuits. If you prefer biscuits with crisp sides like those served by most fast food chains, place biscuits close together but not touching.

Bake for 8 to 10 minutes, or until the tops are golden brown. Serve hot out of the oven. Brush tops with melted butter.

Makes 12 biscuits.

Circa 1900

Beaten Biscuit

Beaten Biscuits were in the original White Lily cookbook. They are more like a cracker than a light biscuit and were favored because they were handy to carry when traveling. The bakers of this bread beat the dough with whatever tool available — hammers, axes, and the like.

2 cups sifted White Lily Flour
1 teaspoon salt
3 tablespoons shortening
Cold water

Sift flour and salt together. Cut or rub in shortening. Add water to make a very stiff dough. Turn out on board and knead until dough holds together. Roll out into long sheet ¼ to ½ inch thick. Fold in thirds and beat with mallet or rolling pin until dough is very thin. Fold the dough over again and repeat until dough looks blistered and satiny smooth (45 to 60 minutes). As the dough becomes sticky during beating, dust it lightly with flour. Then roll out to ¼ to ½ inch thickness. Cut with small biscuit cutter, prick on top, and bake on ungreased baking sheet in slow oven (300° F to 325° F) for 45 minutes to 1 hour.

Yield: about 2 dozen small biscuits.

MEASURING SUCCESS

Measuring flour properly makes a big difference in baking. Flour is packed tightly into bags and packs even more during shipping. Because of this, it needs to be fluffed a little before use. A cup of White Lily Flour weighs about four ounces when measured correctly. If it's packed in the cup, it can weigh about five ounces. This makes a difference in your biscuits. For the best results, follow these steps for measuring flour:

1. Fluff flour a little in the bag or canister by using a spoon or scoop.
2. Spoon flour lightly into the measuring cup.
3. Level flour across the top of the measuring cup by lightly running a metal spatula across it.
4. Pour flour into a mixing bowl. If it stays in the shape of the measuring cup, you know you've packed it too much.

STORING LEFTOVER BISCUITS

Leftover biscuits? Unusual, but it happens. You can seal them in plastic bags or wrap them in foil or plastic wrap once they've cooled. They will keep for a couple of days. Good cooks split, butter and toast leftover biscuits in a broiler or toaster oven. They are excellent crumbled, mixed with corn bread, broth and herbs for poultry stuffing. They also make a decent bread pudding with milk, eggs, sugar and raisins or nuts.

If you want to freeze biscuits, bake them until they are almost done, but not browned. Place cooled biscuits in freezer wrap or bags and freeze. For best results, reheat frozen biscuits at 500° F for two to three minutes. Biscuits can also be warmed in the microwave, but they will lose some of their flaky texture.

Parsley Biscuits with Ham and Honey Mustard

A wedding or reception in the South calls for ham biscuits, usually tiny ones for popping into the mouth with a sip of wine or tea.

2 cups White Lily Self-Rising Flour
½ cup grated Parmesan cheese
2 tablespoons shortening
2 tablespoons butter
3 tablespoons dried whole parsley flakes
⅔ to ¾ cup milk or buttermilk
½ pound thinly sliced cooked ham
Honey Mustard (see page 25)

Preheat oven to 500° F.

Combine flour and Parmesan cheese in a large bowl. Divide the shortening and butter into pieces and scatter them on top of the flour. Work the pieces into the flour with a pastry cutter, two knives, or your fingertips until the pieces are about the size of peas.

Stir in parsley. Add milk or buttermilk gradually, stirring only enough to moisten the flour and hold the dough together.

Turn the dough onto lightly floured surface. Knead gently 2 to 3 strokes. Using a light touch, pat or roll dough to about ⅜-inch thickness. Cut using a 1½-inch floured biscuit cutter, leaving as little dough between cuts as possible. Gather the remaining dough and re-roll one time. Discard remaining scraps.

Place biscuits on a baking sheet close together but not touching.

Bake for 4 to 6 minutes, or until the tops are golden brown. Allow biscuits to cool completely.

Split biscuits in half. Spread bottom half with Honey Mustard. Top with ham and remaining biscuit half.

Makes 20 biscuits.

Circa 1960

Pick-A-Piece Biscuit Loaf

The 1960 White Lily cookbook offered this easy update of the original biscuit recipe.

¾ to 1 cup milk

4 teaspoons instant minced onion

3 cups sifted White Lily Flour

4 teaspoons baking powder

1½ teaspoons salt

1¼ teaspoon dry mustard

⅓ cup shortening

Butter or margarine, melted

Grease 8 x 4-inch loaf pan. Preheat oven to 450° F. Combine ¾ cup milk and onion. In mixing bowl sift together flour, baking powder, salt and mustard. Cut in shortening until mixture resembles coarse crumbs. Blend in milk and onion. Blend in enough milk to make a soft dough. Onto lightly floured board or pastry cloth turn out dough and knead gently 30 seconds. Roll out ½-inch thick. With floured 2¾-inch biscuit cutter, cut out 12 or 13 biscuits. Brush tops with melted butter or margarine. Vertically, on sides, arrange zig-zag fashion, to loosely fill pan. Brush top of loaf with butter or margarine. Bake 25 to 30 minutes, or until top is golden brown. Carefully remove to wire rack and brush again with butter or margarine. Serve warm.

Cheese Drop Biscuits with Garlic Butter

2½ cups White Lily Self-Rising Flour
¼ cup shortening
1 cup shredded cheddar cheese
¾ cup milk or buttermilk
Garlic Butter (see page 25)

Preheat oven to 450° F. Line baking sheet with aluminum foil. Lightly coat foil with nonstick cooking spray.

Measure flour into a large bowl. Divide the shortening into pieces and scatter on top of the flour. Work the pieces into the flour with a pastry cutter, two knives, or your fingertips until they are about the size of peas.

Gradually stir in the cheese and milk or buttermilk, stirring only enough to moisten the flour and hold the dough together.

Drop the biscuits by rounded tablespoons onto baking sheet.

Bake 8 to 10 minutes or until the tops are golden brown. Brush with Garlic Butter. Serve hot out of the oven.

Makes 12 biscuits.

Variations

Cheese Drop Biscuits with Green Chilies: When adding cheese and milk, add 1 (4 ounce) can diced green chilies, very well drained.

Cheese Drop Biscuits with Vidalia Onion: When adding cheese and milk, add ¼ cup of finely chopped Vidalia onion.

Sweet Potato Biscuits with Orange Honey Butter

Select dark orange sweet potatoes because they are sweeter than the pale yellow ones. They are usually grown in North Carolina and Louisiana. Flavored butter with the biscuits makes a special teatime treat or dessert.

1 cup White Lily Self-Rising Flour

⅛ teaspoon ground cinnamon

1 tablespoon brown sugar

½ teaspoon baking powder

4 tablespoons butter

1 (15 ounce) can sweet potatoes or 1 large sweet potato, cooked and peeled

Orange Honey Butter (see page 25)

Preheat oven to 450° F. Spray baking sheet with nonstick cooking spray.

In a large bowl, combine flour, cinnamon, brown sugar, and baking powder. Divide the butter into pieces and scatter on top of the flour. Work the pieces into the flour with a pastry cutter, two knives, or your fingertips until the pieces are about the size of peas. Mash enough sweet potatoes to measure ¾ cup. Add, stirring only enough to moisten the flour and hold the dough together.

Turn the dough onto lightly floured surface. Knead gently 2 to 3 strokes. Using a light touch, pat or roll to about ½-inch thickness. Cut biscuits using a floured 2-inch cutter, leaving as little dough between cuts as possible. Gather the remaining dough and re-roll one time. Discard remaining scraps.

Place biscuits on baking sheet with sides touching for soft Southern-style biscuits. If you prefer biscuits with crisp sides like those served by most fast-food chains, place biscuits on the baking sheet close together but not touching.

Bake for 10 to 12 minutes, or until tops are browned. Serve hot out of the oven. Split biscuits in half and fill with Orange Honey Butter.

Makes 10 biscuits.

"LIGHT" BISCUITS SECRET UNCOVERED

Keep in mind that making light biscuits takes a little practice. If they aren't perfect the first time, review these tips and make adjustments in your technique.

Divide the shortening into pieces and scatter it in the bowl, coating each piece with flour. This prevents the shortening from bunching up on the cutting tool. Work chunks of shortening into the flour with a pastry cutter, two knives, or your fingertips until the pieces are about the size of peas. If you use your fingers, work quickly or the heat from your hands will melt the shortening. When the shortening melts, biscuits are not flaky.

Stir only until the milk is blended. Overstirring makes biscuits tough.

Although most recipes will tell you to knead the dough, gently folding it a few times is plenty. Handling the dough too much will make your biscuits tough.

Lightly sprinkle flour on your rolling pin, your biscuit cutter, and the surface you plan to place your dough on. Use only enough flour to keep the dough from sticking.

Dip the cutter into the flour between each biscuit. For evenly shaped biscuits with straight sides, press the cutter straight down without twisting.

Brush the tops of your biscuits with melted butter once they've finished baking to make them shinier.

Biscuit Toppings

Grandma's Gravy

Biscuits and gravy are a weekend treat at Grandma's house for many Southerners. The children stay cuddled in bed until they smell the bacon and sausage frying. Then it's a race to see who gets to the kitchen first. You can use a different combination of meats to get the base for this gravy, but the one here works the best.

8 slices bacon

4 sausage patties

⅓ cup plus 1 tablespoon White Lily Plain All-Purpose Flour

1¼ teaspoons salt, or to taste

3½ cups milk, room temperature

Cook meat in large, heavy skillet until brown and crispy. Remove meat and drain on paper towels. Add flour to grease remaining in skillet and stir over medium-high heat until slightly brown, about 1 minute. Add salt and milk. Stir constantly until gravy begins to thicken, about 10 minutes. Serve over biscuits, with bacon and sausage.

Makes enough gravy for 12 biscuits.

Flavored butters make special toppings for biscuits, pancakes, and vegetables. Orange honey butter is excellent on broccoli or carrots.

Blackberry Butter

8 tablespoons (1 stick) butter, softened
¼ cup blackberry jam

Blend and serve. Store in the refrigerator.

Orange Honey Butter

4 tablespoons butter or margarine, softened
2 tablespoons honey
1 teaspoon grated orange zest

Combine ingredients.
Cover and refrigerate until needed.

Honey Mustard

½ cup mayonnaise
3 tablespoons whole-grain mustard
2 tablespoons honey
1 teaspoon grated orange zest
¼ teaspoon allspice

Combine ingredients.
Cover and refrigerate until needed.

Garlic Butter

4 tablespoons butter, softened
½ teaspoon garlic powder
1 tablespoon fresh chopped parsley, optional

Blend and serve. Store in the refrigerator.

Cinnamon Molasses Butter

8 tablespoons (1 stick) butter, softened
2 to 3 tablespoons molasses, or to taste
½ teaspoon ground cinnamon

Blend and serve. Store in the refrigerator.

Corn Bread

There's no sweeter sound than corn bread batter starting to sizzle as it's poured from the mixing bowl into the hot oil used to grease the pan. Corn bread crackling in a cast-iron skillet sings a song of perfection and delight.

While the rest of the country seems to prefer wheat-based breads these days, people in the South are still partial to life-sustaining corn. Corn bread has been a tradition for as long as folks can remember.

Jeanne Voltz, a well-known Southern cookbook author, remembers sitting on the tall back steps of her house munching her after-school snack: corn bread left from dinner, split and filled with spring onions just pulled from her dad's garden, and washing it all down with a cold glass of fresh, sweet buttermilk. Others remember dinners of hot buttered corn sticks with fresh-cooked green beans.

Originally, corn was called maize, a word that means universal mother or life-sustaining force. That it truly was. For more than six thousand years, corn and the breads made from it have sustained all Americans. For Native Americans, corn played a major role in their lives. It was eaten as a vegetable, boiled like a grain, and ground for bread. Its sugar was extracted to make sweet confections. Corn stalks were used to build houses, corn silks for medicine, and cobs as fuel.

For the early colonists, corn meant the difference between life and death. With help from Native Americans, settlers to the New World quickly realized the usefulness and versatility of corn. Several hundred years later, corn and cornmeal would once again be a shield protecting against starvation as Southerners struggled through the terrible times of the Civil

War and Reconstruction.

Using whole-grain, stone-ground corn, early cooks mixed this coarse version of cornmeal with a little water, salt and grease to create baked goods. It wasn't long before they found new ways of making this basic bread. Soon, they had progressed from ashcakes (baked in fireplace ashes) to hoecakes (fried on a piece of metal such as a hoe) to corn pones (baked in a makeshift oven). By the sixteenth century, cooks had learned how to combine potassium carbonate (which wood ash was sometimes used to provide) or bicarbonate of soda with sour milk to create corn bread as it's known today.

These days cooks are saved the time and trouble of grinding their own corn or even of adding baking soda to their cornmeal. Good cooks know the best crusty corn bread with light and moist insides is made with whole kernel cornmeal. White Lily Cornmeal Mix is ground from whole kernel corn, which gives it a good flavor and makes it good for you, too. Many mills remove the bran and germ, but not White Lily. With a little soft wheat flour added in, their cornmeal makes every pan of corn bread rise higher and be melt-in-your-mouth tender.

White Lily Southern Corn Bread

The great corn bread controversy is over whether it should be sweet. Some think so, while others strongly disagree. We've made the sugar optional so you can make your corn bread just the way you like it. Many people take care of the issue by spreading their corn bread with honey or molasses.

1¼ to 1½ cups milk or buttermilk

¼ cup vegetable oil

1 large egg, lightly beaten

2 cups White Lily Self-Rising Cornmeal Mix

1 to 2 tablespoons sugar, optional

Preheat oven to 425° F. Grease an 8- or 10-inch cast-iron skillet or an 8 x 8 x 2-inch baking pan. Place cast-iron skillet in oven to preheat.

Combine milk, oil, and egg in a large bowl. Add cornmeal mix and, if desired, sugar. Stir just until moistened. (Batter should be lumpy.)

Pour batter into preheated skillet or pan. Bake for 20 to 25 minutes for 10-inch skillet or 25 to 30 minutes for 8-inch skillet or pan, or until golden brown. Cut into wedges and serve hot out of the oven.

Makes 8 servings.

Variations

Muffins: Fill greased muffin cups two-thirds full, Bake at 425° F for 20 to 25 minutes. Makes 16 muffins.

Corn Sticks: Preheat well-greased, heavy corn stick pans. Fill almost full. Bake at 425° F for 12 to 16 minutes. Makes 16 to 18 corn sticks.

Buttery Corn Bread: Substitute 8 tablespoons (1 stick) melted butter or margarine for ¼ cup vegetable oil. Mix and bake as directed.

Low-Cholesterol Corn Bread: Use skim milk, vegetable oil, and substitute 2 egg whites or ¼ cup egg substitute for the egg. Mix and bake as directed.

Low-Fat Corn Bread: Use skim milk, 1 tablespoon dried butter substitute, 2 tablespoons unsweetened applesauce, ¼ cup egg substitute or 2 egg whites. Mix and bake as directed.

Double Corn Muffins

1 small onion, chopped (½ to 1 cup)

2 tablespoons butter

1 (8½ ounce) can creamed corn

¼ cup milk

1 large egg, lightly beaten

¼ cup sour cream

1½ cups White Lily Self-Rising Cornmeal Mix

1 to 2 tablespoons sugar, optional

Preheat oven to 350° F. Lightly grease 12 muffin cups.

Sauté onions in butter until tender. Or melt butter in microwave, stir in chopped onions, and microwave on high (100 percent power) 2 to 3 minutes or until onions are tender. Set aside, allowing onions to cool.

Combine corn, milk, egg, sour cream, and cooled onion in a large bowl. Add cornmeal mix and, if desired, sugar. Stir until just moistened. (Batter should be lumpy.)

Fill muffin cups two-thirds full. Bake for 25 to 30 minutes or until browned. Serve muffins hot out of the oven.

Makes 12 muffins.

Jalapeño Corn Bread

When chicken or steaks come off the backyard grill, pass wedges or squares of this freshly baked bread. Jalapeños originated in the Americas and they aren't really the hottest peppers, especially if you remove the seeds and pulp. If jalapeños are still too hot for your tastes, try larger peppers such as Anaheim.

2 large eggs, lightly beaten

½ cup (4 ounces) sour cream

1 (8½ ounce) can creamed corn

2 medium jalapeño peppers, diced (or to taste)

¼ cup onion, diced

¼ cup red pepper, diced

2¼ cups White Lily Self-Rising Cornmeal Mix

2 tablespoons sugar, optional

Preheat oven to 425° F. Grease or add oil to a 10-inch cast-iron skillet. Place skillet in oven to preheat.

Blend eggs, sour cream, corn, jalapeño peppers, onion, and red pepper in a large bowl. Add cornmeal mix and, if desired, sugar. Stir just until moistened. (This mixture will be thick.)

Pour into preheated skillet. Bake for 20 to 25 minutes. Cut into wedges and serve hot out of the oven.

Makes 8 servings.

Variation

Jalapeño Corn Bread with Cheese: Add 1 cup cheddar cheese to egg mixture. Mix and bake as directed.

Circa 1920

Corn Meal Muffins

This recipe was created before White Lily milled cornmeal mix. Now it's much simpler to make this old-timey muffin. Just omit the first five ingredients and add 2 cups of White Lily Self-Rising Cornmeal Mix.

½ cup sifted White Lily Flour

1½ cups water ground meal

1 teaspoon salt

1 teaspoon baking powder

½ teaspoon soda

1 tablespoon sugar

1 egg or 2 egg yolks

1 cup fresh buttermilk

2 tablespoons melted shortening

Sift flour, meal, salt, baking powder, soda, and sugar together. Beat egg and add buttermilk and shortening. Add to flour mixture. Fill greased muffin pans ⅔ full and bake in moderately hot oven (425°F) 20 to 25 minutes.

Yield: 20 to 22 small muffins.

Sour Cream and Vidalia Onion Corn Bread

1 large Vidalia or other sweet onion, thinly sliced with slices cut in half or quartered
2 tablespoons butter
1 large egg, lightly beaten
⅓ cup milk
2 tablespoons vegetable oil
2 cups White Lily Self-Rising Cornmeal Mix
1 to 2 tablespoons sugar, optional
½ cup sour cream
¼ teaspoon dried basil, optional

Preheat oven to 350° F. Grease or add oil to a 12-inch cast-iron skillet or 12-inch baking pan. Place cast iron skillet in oven to preheat.

Sauté onions in butter or margarine until tender or melt butter in microwave and stir in onions. Microwave on high (100 percent power) 2 to 3 minutes or until onions are tender. Set aside, allowing to cool.

Combine egg, milk, and oil in a large bowl. Add cornmeal mix and, if desired, sugar. Stir until just moistened. (Batter should be lumpy.)

Combine sautéed onion with sour cream and basil. Spread half of cornmeal batter in preheated skillet or pan. Top with onion mixture. Then layer with remaining cornmeal batter.

Bake for 22 to 27 minutes or until golden brown.

Makes 8 servings.

CRAZY 'BOUT CORN BREAD: CORNBREAD COOKING TIPS

The secret to good corn bread is to mix it with a light hand and cook it in a hot pan. Here are some other tips to help you cook your corn bread just right:

Use whole kernel cornmeal. The whole kernel contains natural corn oil. It makes your bread taste like fresh sweet corn. Many mills remove the bran and germ, which removes the flavorful parts of the corn and leaves basically corn flour. White Lily packs coarsely ground, whole kernel cornmeal into every bag and blends it with all the ingredients you need for making perfect, full-flavored corn bread every time.

Measure cornmeal the same way you measure flour. See page 18. Mix the batter until all the ingredients are moist. The batter will not be smooth. Avoid overmixing or your corn bread will be tough and have tunnels and peaked tops. Preheat the pan for crispy corn bread edges. Use a cast-iron skillet and pour in a little corn oil or bacon grease. The pan will sizzle when the corn bread batter is added, and your corn bread will have a crisp, brown crust on its sides and bottom.

CARING FOR CAST IRON

When it comes to cooking corn bread, it is well worth the effort to season a cast-iron skillet. Corn bread cooked in cast iron has a crispy crunchy outside and a moist buttery inside. Here are some tips on how to get the most service out of your cast-iron skillet.

1. Wash your new skillet with soap and water. This will be the first and last time that you do. 2. Dry the skillet and rub the surface with a paper towel dipped in shortening or vegetable oil. 3. Put it in a 250° F oven for several hours. The oil will turn dark brown. Although your skillet is now ready for cooking, the flavor will continue to improve with time. 4. Care for your seasoned skillet by simply wiping it off with a damp or dry cloth. Washing it with soap and water will undo the "seasoning" of the skillet. Dry well, and re-coat with oil between uses. 5. Pour a little oil in the pan each time you cook. This will keep food from sticking to the skillet.

Broccoli Corn Bread

One of the most popular vegetables, broccoli is a great way to add vitamins A and C to a meal.

1¼ cups milk or buttermilk
¼ cup vegetable oil
2 large eggs, lightly beaten
2 cups White Lily Self-Rising Cornmeal Mix
¼ teaspoon onion powder
¼ teaspoon freshly ground black pepper
1½ cups shredded cheddar cheese
2 cups finely chopped broccoli or 1 small package frozen chopped broccoli, thawed

Preheat oven to 425° F. Grease or add oil to an 8- or 10-inch cast-iron skillet or 9-inch baking pan. Place skillet in oven to preheat.

   Combine milk or buttermilk, oil, and eggs in a large bowl. Add cornmeal mix, onion powder, and black pepper. Stir until just moistened. Fold in cheese and broccoli. Pour batter into preheated skillet or pan.

   Bake for 25 to 30 minutes. Cut into wedges and serve hot out of the oven.

Makes 8 servings.

Corn Bread with Cheese and Spinach

1¼ cups milk or buttermilk

¼ cup vegetable oil

1 large egg, lightly beaten

2 cups White Lily Self-Rising Cornmeal Mix

¼ teaspoon garlic powder

¼ teaspoon onion powder

¼ teaspoon freshly ground black pepper

¼ cup grated Parmesan cheese

1 (9 ounce) package frozen spinach, thawed

1½ cups shredded cheddar cheese

Preheat oven to 425° F. Grease or add oil to an 8- or 10-inch cast-iron skillet or 9-inch baking pan. Place skillet in oven to preheat.

Combine milk or buttermilk, oil, and egg in a large bowl. Add cornmeal mix, garlic powder, onion powder, black pepper, and Parmesan cheese. Stir until just moistened. (Batter should be lumpy.)

Fold in spinach and cheddar cheese. Pour batter into preheated skillet or pan. Bake for 20 to 25 minutes.

Makes 8 servings.

Circa 1930

Cracklin' Bread

The best barbecue joints in the South still serve their corn pones and corn bread with the added crunch and flavor of cracklings. Cracklings are the crisp tidbits made from sautéing pork to extract most of the fat. The original cracklings were the crisp remains of boiling lard.

1 cup (4 ounces) finely diced pork fat or salt pork
2 cups White Lily Self-Rising Cornmeal Mix
1 cup buttermilk
2 eggs, beaten
Preheat oven to 425° F.

Grease 10-inch oven-going skillet; set aside. To make cracklings, rinse pork fat; pat dry. In another skillet, fry pork fat until crisp. Drain, reserving ⅓ cup drippings. Add oil if necessary to make ⅓ cup. In mixing bowl, stir together cornmeal mix, buttermilk, eggs and the reserved drippings; beat until smooth. Stir in cracklings. Turn into prepared skillet. Bake in 425° F oven for 15 to 20 minutes or till done. Cut into wedges. Serve warm.

Makes 6 servings.

Salsa Corn Bread

This cornbread recipe is excellent mixed with vegetables in a Mediterranean-style Corn Bread Salad (see page 95), or it is an easy way to spice up any meal.

1 tablespoon plus 1 teaspoon vegetable oil

1½ cups White Lily Self-Rising Cornmeal Mix

½ teaspoon garlic powder

½ teaspoon cayenne pepper, optional

1 (4 ounce) can diced green chilies, drained

1 large egg, lightly beaten

½ cup milk

½ cup salsa

Preheat oven to 425° F. Add 1 teaspoon vegetable oil to an 8- to 10-inch skillet or baking pan and place in oven to preheat.

In a large bowl, stir together cornmeal mix and garlic. Add cayenne pepper if desired. In a separate bowl, mix 1 tablespoon vegetable oil, chilies, egg, milk, and salsa. Pour this mixture into the cornmeal mixture. Stir just until blended. Pour into preheated pan.

If using 8-inch pan, bake 30 to 35 minutes. If using 10-inch pan, bake 25 to 30 minutes.

Makes 8 servings.

Hush Puppies

Legend has it that this name comes from tossing bits of fried-fish breading to the dogs to get them to hush their howling. That may not be true, but it is a fact that it isn't a fish fry without hush puppies alongside.

Vegetable oil for deep-fat frying
1½ cups White Lily Self-Rising Cornmeal Mix
⅔ cup milk
1 large egg, lightly beaten
¼ cup finely chopped onion

In deep saucepan or fryer, heat oil to 375° F. In large bowl, combine cornmeal mix, milk and egg. Stir until just blended. Stir in onion.

   Drop by rounded teaspoonfuls, a few at a time, into hot oil. Fry for 2 minutes, or until golden brown, turning once. Drain on paper towels.

Makes 20 hush puppies.

Variation

Cajun Hush Puppies: Add the following seasonings to mix before stirring in onion: ½ teaspoon cayenne pepper, ½ teaspoon thyme leaves, ¼ teaspoon white pepper, ¼ teaspoon black pepper, ⅛ teaspoon oregano leaves, and 1 minced garlic clove. Substitute green onions for white. Prepare and cook as directed.

Quick Breads and Muffins

Dainty sandwiches of banana bread sliced thin and spread with cream cheese or soft butter, chicken salad spooned into a tiny tart, a cucumber sandwich, and a slice of melon — not so long ago, this was a hostess's favorite plate for her sewing or garden club, the fanciest ladies' lunch she served. And husbands and sons adored the leftovers.

Banana bread is probably the most well known of all the quick breads. Cooks like it because it gives them something useful to do with bananas past their prime. Everyone else delights in these breads because they taste so wonderful. Moist and filled with fruit, a loaf of quick bread sitting beside the coffee pot in the office break room disappears quickly. Quick breads welcome new neighbors and serve as holiday gifts.

One simple secret to perfectly baked quick breads is to bake them the day before you plan to serve them. Once you take the bread from the oven and let it cool, wrap it tightly in foil or plastic film. This makes the bread easier to slice. It will also prevent the bread from being crumbly or mushy in the center. Waiting a day gives the bread time to set and allows the flavors to blend. However, it's nearly impossible to do, as the sweet, heady smell of fresh fruit bread will drive even the most self-controlled people to distraction. One bite and all is lost. It's not uncommon for a whole loaf to disappear within an hour.

Instead of the rising time and kneading that yeast bread requires, quick breads rely on baking powder, baking soda, steam, air, or a combination of these to make dough rise. That's how these breads can be ready in such a hurry.

Muffins are very similar in texture and taste to quick breads. In fact, some quick bread batters can be baked as muffins or slightly sweet tea breads. However, not every quick bread batter will make a smooth switch to muffin mix and vice versa, so be sure to experiment before you try this trick for company. Hot muffins are a perfect dinner bread when you want a change from corn bread or biscuits.

In the early days, muffins were called "gems." Meaning perfect specimen, "gem" is truly an appropriate name for the much-loved muffin. The name change from gem to muffin may have reflected this quick bread's ability to warm the hands, much as knitted muffs do, especially if the bread is rushed right from the oven to eager hands around the table.

Banana Nut Bread

Slice and spread with cream cheese or butter for picnics and snacks.

2½ cups White Lily Plain All-Purpose Flour

1 teaspoon salt

1 teaspoon baking soda

½ cup vegetable shortening

2 cups sugar

2 cups mashed ripe banana (4 or 5 bananas)

3 large eggs, lightly beaten

½ cup chopped walnuts, black walnuts, or pecans

1 teaspoon pure vanilla extract

Preheat oven to 350° F. Grease the bottoms only of two 8½ x 4½ x 2½-inch loaf pans.

Combine flour, salt, and baking soda in a small bowl. In a mixing bowl, combine shortening, sugar, mashed banana, eggs, nuts, and vanilla, and beat until well blended. Add the dry ingredients and stir just until moistened. Pour into prepared pan.

Bake for 60 to 65 minutes, or until a toothpick inserted in the center comes out clean. Remove from oven and let cool in the pan for 10 minutes. Remove from pan and cool on wire rack.

Makes 2 loaves.

Pumpkin 'n' Spice Bread

With self-rising flour and a can of pumpkin, this recipe couldn't be easier.

3½ cups White Lily Self-Rising Flour

1 teaspoon ground cinnamon

½ teaspoon ground cloves

½ teaspoon ground allspice

½ teaspoon nutmeg

2½ cups granulated sugar

½ cup packed brown sugar

1 cup vegetable oil

4 large eggs, lightly beaten

1 (16 ounce) can solid pack pumpkin

Preheat oven to 350° F. Grease and flour the bottom only of two 9 x 5 x 3-inch loaf pans.

Combine flour, cinnamon, cloves, allspice, and nutmeg in a small bowl. In a mixing bowl, combine granulated sugar, brown sugar, oil, and eggs. Beat until well blended. Add pumpkin; blend well. Pour batter into prepared pans.

Bake for 55 minutes, or until toothpick inserted in the center comes out clean. Remove from oven and let cool in the pan for 15 minutes. Remove from pans and cool on wire rack.

Makes 2 loaves.

If a child or grandchild is anxious to try baking, quick breads are a great place to start. They are virtually foolproof — with a few cautions:

Don't overmix the batter or the breads will be tough and muffins will be laced with tunnels. Mix the dry ingredients in a bowl. Combine eggs and liquid in a measuring cup or small bowl, pour into a well in the flour mixture, and stir in lightly.

For a golden brown crust, bake muffins in shiny aluminum muffin pans. Dark pans may give the crusts a scorched look.

Grease only the bottoms of muffin cups.

Baking two loaves of fruit or nut breads at a time is efficient. Quick breads freeze well, and you can thaw a loaf for some busy day when you need a special bread. Cool the bread thoroughly, wrap in a layer of plastic wrap, then wrap in a sheet of foil or slip into a freezer bag. Muffins can be wrapped and frozen this way, too. To thaw, remove from the freezer and leave at room temperature.

Fruits and nuts can add variety to a good recipe for muffins. Fruits should be washed and dried well before adding to the batter so that they do not make it too thin. Raisins and most other dried fruits can be stirred into the batter with no problems, but avoid juicy fruits, except in recipes tested for these additions. If using frozen blueberries, add them to the dough while still frozen and fold in lightly or the bread may turn a murky gray color. Fruits and nuts will be distributed more evenly if tossed with a couple of tablespoonfuls of the flour called for in the recipe and folded in lightly after the batter is mixed.

Blueberry Muffins with Streusel Topping

Blueberries are at the height of their season when the middle of the summer sets in the South. These muffins are a sweet offering to overnight guests on a hot Sunday morning. Or for dessert, split the muffins and top with a scoop of ice cream or fruit yogurt.

1 cup blueberries

2 cups White Lily Self-Rising Flour

⅓ cup sugar

¾ cup milk

1 large egg, lightly beaten

¼ cup vegetable oil

Streusel Topping

2 tablespoons White Lily Self-Rising Flour

2 tablespoons sugar

1 tablespoon butter, softened

Preheat oven to 400° F. Grease bottoms only of 12 muffin cups or line with paper baking cups.

Make the Streusel Topping by combining the flour, sugar, and butter until crumbly. Set aside.

Rinse, drain, and thoroughly dry blueberries on paper towels. Combine flour and sugar. Toss blueberries in ¼ cup of flour mixture.

Whisk milk, egg, and oil together until blended. Add liquid ingredients to flour mixture and stir 5 to 7 strokes (batter will not be completely mixed). Fold in floured blueberries. Stir only until ingredients are moistened. Batter will be lumpy. Do not overmix.

Fill prepared muffin cups two-thirds to three-fourths full with batter. Sprinkle tops with streusel. Bake for 15 to 18 minutes, or until golden brown.

Makes 12 muffins.

Circa 1950

Muffins

This muffin recipe from the 1950s edition of the White Lily cookbook is versatile enough for all occasions — and easy, too. You can vary this basic recipe by adding ½ cup minced crisp bacon; 1 cup grated cheese and ¼ cup milk; ¾ cup nuts or currants; or 1 cup apples with sugar and cinnamon.

2 cups White Lily Flour	1 egg
1 tablespoon baking powder	1 cup milk
1 teaspoon salt	3 tablespoons melted shortening or
2 tablespoons sugar	salad oil

Heat oven to 400° F. Grease bottoms of muffin-pan cups with shortening.

Stir flour, baking powder, salt, and sugar together in a medium bowl to mix well. Make a "well" in the center. In a 2-cup measuring cup or a small bowl, beat egg. Stir in milk and shortening. Pour all at once into "well" in flour mixture. Mix quickly and lightly with fork until all the flour is moistened, but do not beat. The batter will be lumpy.

Fill muffin cups two-thirds full with batter. Wipe off any spilled batter. Bake in center of oven 25 minutes, or until muffins are golden brown. Remove from oven and place on a wire rack. Run a spatula around the outside edge of each muffin to loosen. Lift out and serve at once.

Makes 12 muffins.

Mocha Chocolate Chip Muffins with Pecan Streusel Topping

Who said muffins can't be chocolate?

2 cups White Lily Self-Rising Flour
½ cup granulated sugar
1 teaspoon cinnamon
¾ cup (4 ounces) semisweet chocolate chips
2 large eggs, lightly beaten
⅓ cup milk
½ cup vegetable oil
¼ cup brown sugar
1 tablespoon instant coffee dissolved in 1 teaspoon boiling water

Pecan Streusel Topping

¼ cup White Lily Self-Rising Flour
1 teaspoon ground cinnamon
¼ cup brown sugar
3 tablespoons butter, softened
1 cup chopped pecans

Preheat oven to 375° F. Lightly grease the bottoms only of 12 muffin cups or line with paper baking cups.

Make the Pecan Streusel Topping by combining flour, cinnamon, sugar, butter, and pecans until crumbly. Set aside.

Combine flour, granulated sugar, and cinnamon in a large bowl. Toss in the chocolate chips.

Combine eggs, milk, oil, brown sugar, and coffee mixture in a medium bowl. Pour the liquid mixture over the flour mixture. Stir only until ingredients are moistened. Batter will be lumpy. Do not overmix.

Fill prepared muffin cups two-thirds to three-fourths full with batter. Sprinkle tops with pecan streusel. Bake for 12 to 15 minutes, or until golden brown.

Makes 12 muffins.

Lemon Poppy Seed Muffins

Serve these with omelets for an appetizing brunch. When grating the lemon peel, be sure to use only the yellow, not the white, part of the peel. The white part is bitter.

1½ cups White Lily Self-Rising Flour

¼ cup sugar

2 to 3 tablespoons poppy seeds

¼ cup plus 2 tablespoons milk

1 teaspoon grated lemon zest

2 tablespoons fresh lemon juice

1 large egg, lightly beaten

⅓ cup vegetable oil

Lemon Sugar Topping

¼ cup sugar

1 teaspoon grated lemon zest

Preheat oven to 400° F.

Grease the bottoms only of 12 muffin cups or line with paper baking cups.

Make the Lemon Sugar Topping by combining the sugar and grated lemon zest. Set aside.

In a mixing bowl, combine flour, sugar, and poppy seeds. In another bowl, combine milk, lemon zest, lemon juice, egg, and oil. Add to flour mixture. Stir only until all ingredients are moistened. Batter will be lumpy.

Fill prepared muffin cups two-thirds to three-fourths full with batter. Sprinkle with topping. Bake for 12 to 15 minutes or until golden brown.

Makes 12 muffins.

Circa 1950

Spiced Plum Loaf

White Lily brochures were passed out in the 1950s with fast and easy recipes, including this unique sweet bread.

1 cup oil	2 cups White Lily Self-Rising Flour
2 cups sugar	1 teaspoon cloves
3 eggs	1 teaspoon cinnamon
2 small jars strained plums	½ teaspoon allspice
(baby food)	½ teaspoon nutmeg

Preheat oven to 325° F. Grease and flour two 9 x 5-inch bread pans. Cream oil, sugar, and eggs together. Beat in strained plums. Combine remaining ingredients and add to batter. Mix well. Pour into prepared pans. Bake 60 minutes.

Makes one loaf.

Apricot-Orange Bread

1 cup chopped dried apricots

2 cups boiling water

2 cups White Lily Plain All-Purpose Flour

¾ cup sugar

1½ teaspoons baking powder

1 teaspoon salt

½ teaspoon baking soda

¾ cup orange juice

1 egg, beaten

2 tablespoons vegetable oil

2 teaspoons grated fresh orange peel

½ cup chopped pecans

Glaze

½ cup sifted confectioners' sugar

1 to 2 teaspoons orange juice

Grated fresh orange peel, optional

Preheat oven to 350° F. Lightly grease one 8 x 4 x 2-inch loaf pan.

In small bowl, cover apricots with boiling water. Set aside.

In mixing bowl, combine flour, sugar, baking powder, salt, and baking soda. Combine ¾ cup orange juice, egg, oil, and 2 teaspoons orange peel. Add orange juice mixture to flour mixture, stirring just until moistened.

Drain apricots thoroughly. Fold apricots and pecans into batter. Spoon batter into prepared pan.

Bake for 50 to 60 minutes, or until toothpick inserted in the center comes out clean. Remove from oven and let cool in the pan for 10 minutes. Remove from pan and cool completely on wire rack.

To make glaze, blend confectioners' sugar with 1 teaspoon orange juice. Add additional orange juice until drizzling consistency. Drizzle glaze over loaf. Sprinkle grated orange peel over glaze, if desired.

Makes 1 large loaf.

Pancakes and Waffles

The peaceful call of mockingbirds and the soft ray of sunlight dancing on your pillow signal the arrival of a leisurely weekend. You're well-rested, relaxed, and nothing sounds better than brewing a cup of coffee and making light and fluffy pancakes or crispy waffles for your family.

Pancakes have been called griddlecakes, batter cakes, hoecakes, and flapjacks, and they are one of mankind's oldest forms of bread. Most people think of them as breakfast cakes, but they make an interesting and delicious dinner bread, too. The choice of toppers is infinite. The standard in states such as Alabama used to be cane or sorghum molasses. Honey is an option, or pure maple syrup from Vermont, Maine, or the Appalachian mountains.

Waffles make as good a dessert as they do a breakfast. For folks with a sweet tooth that won't stop, waffles have an advantage over pancakes. Their square pockets are perfect for soaking in syrup, bathing with butter, or filling with fruit.

A contribution of creative Dutch colonists, the waffle had become a national craze by the end of the eighteenth century. Waffle parties were all the rage.

Pancakes and waffles are often a Sunday Best Breakfast, with Dad taking over flipping pancakes on the griddle while Mom gets ready for church. Although nowadays pancakes and waffles are easy to prepare in the morning, you can mix up the batter the night before.

Many nineteenth century cookbooks actually recommend an overnight rest for batter. In 1889, Estelle Wilcox explained in *The New Dixie Cook-Book*, "All griddle-cakes are much nicer mixed and kept overnight, to allow the flour to swell, stirring in the whites of eggs and soda or baking powder, when used, just before baking." And although in 1847 Eliza Leslie in *Miss Leslie's New Cooking Book* suggests that you "Cover the pan and set it on the dresser till morning," it's a much safer bet just to store it in the fridge.

The silky texture and low protein content of soft wheat flour ensures that that your pancakes will be light and fluffy and your waffles crispy and crunchy.

The All-Time Favorite Pancakes

In the original White Lily cookbook, pancakes were called batter cakes. But other than that, the recipe hasn't changed much. We've cut the oil by one-third, and we have made the recipe smaller. After publishing many variations to this recipe over the years, we know this one is really the all-time favorite.

1¼ cups White Lily Self-Rising Flour
2 tablespoons sugar
1 cup milk (see note)
1 large egg, lightly beaten
1 tablespoon vegetable oil

Preheat lightly greased griddle to 400° F. In mixing bowl, combine flour and sugar. In another small bowl, combine milk, egg, and oil. Add liquid ingredients to flour mixture, stirring just until the ingredients are moistened. Batter will be slightly lumpy.

Pour ¼ cup batter onto hot griddle for each standard-size pancake. Cook until golden brown, turning once. Serve with butter or margarine and syrup or with Toasted Walnut Butter (see page 59).

Makes eight 4-inch pancakes.

Note: Increase the milk for thinner pancakes or decrease for thicker pancakes.

Variations

Fruit Pancakes: Fold into batter 1 cup of blueberries, strawberries, peach slices, or other soft fruits.

Nut Pancakes: Fold into batter 1 cup walnuts or pecans. Nuts can also be added to the syrup and poured over pancakes.

Chocolate Chip Pancakes: Fold into batter 1 cup of semisweet mini-morsels. Sprinkle pancake tops with confectioners' sugar.

Circa 1930

Green Corn Griddle Cakes

Botanically, when sweet corn is ready to be picked and eaten, it's not "ripe." Hence the name green corn. Either grate fresh corn or use canned creamed corn for this recipe. These cakes are designed to serve with fried chicken at dinner, but they are also good topped with salsa, guacamole, or sour cream.

2 Cups grated corn pulp	1 Teaspoon salt
1 Cup milk	2 Cups White Lily Flour
2 Well beaten eggs	4 Teaspoons baking powder
4 Tablespoons sugar	2 Tablesp'ns melted shortening

Mix well, beat until thoroughly blended. Bake on hot, lightly greased griddle. Serve with fried chicken.

PANCAKE POINTERS

Heat griddle to 400° F before using. Drop a couple of drops of water on the griddle to see if they "dance." If they do, your griddle is ready for cooking. Use a non-stick pan or griddle to reduce the amount of fat needed for cooking.

Blend dry ingredients only until they are moistened. Batter will be lumpy.

For uniform-sized pancakes, use a ¼ measuring cup, or better yet, an ice-cream scoop to dip the batter.

Turn pancakes when the top bubbles and sides start to appear dry. Turn only once.

For light and tall pancakes, let them rise on the griddle without pressing the top. Pressing the spatula on the top of the pancakes makes them, as the old saying goes, "flat as a pancake."

For a nutrition boost, add fruit to the batter or to the top of the pancakes. Children love to make fruit faces. Slice a banana for the mouth and put strawberries for eyes. If you don't mind a little mess, let them experiment with their own designs. It makes pancakes all the more fun to eat.

To serve everyone at the same time: Place pancakes on a baking sheet and cover with a lint-free cloth. Store in a 200° F oven.

To store pancakes, freeze them between layers of wax paper in an airtight container. They will keep for up to three months. To reheat, microwave on medium for about 2 minutes or bake at 300° F for 10 minutes.

Cornmeal Pancakes

Cornmeal pancakes are a great eye-opener in the morning and a hearty supper bread served with bacon or thin grilled pork chops for a fast meal after a busy day.

2 cups White Lily Self-Rising Cornmeal Mix
2 large eggs, lightly beaten
2¼ cups buttermilk (see note)
2 tablespoons butter, melted

Preheat lightly greased griddle to 400° F. Combine cornmeal mix, eggs, buttermilk, and butter, stirring just until the ingredients are moistened. Batter will be slightly lumpy.

Pour ¼ cup batter onto hot griddle for each standard-size pancake. Cook until golden brown, turning once. Serve with butter or margarine and syrup.

Makes eight 4-inch pancakes.

Note: Increase the buttermilk for thinner pancakes or decrease for thicker pancakes.

Toasted Walnut Butter

½ pound (2 sticks) butter, softened

½ cup finely chopped toasted walnuts

2 tablespoons confectioners' sugar

¼ teaspoon maple flavoring

¼ teaspoon pure vanilla extract

In small bowl, combine all ingredients. Blend well.

Makes 1 ½ cups.

WAFFLE WISDOM

Waffles are a fun version of pancakes. Their crisp exterior has a pattern of ridges that hold the butter, syrup, and other toppings securely in place.
For wonderful waffles, remember these tips:

Make sure the batter is thicker than pancake batter.

Cook waffles until the waffle iron no longer steams around the edges.

Waffles are done when the exterior is a crispy golden brown. They are best when eaten immediately.

Store waffles by freezing them between layers of wax paper in an airtight container. Reheat in a 350° F oven for 5 minutes. Reheat for about one minute in a microwave or two minutes in a toaster.

Best-Ever White Lily Waffles

Waffles are for those who want ridges to hold their syrup in place. This recipe will provide perfection every time. For dessert one night, add crushed pecans to the batter and serve the waffles with sliced fruit, whipped topping, nutmeg, and honey.

1 cup White Lily Self-Rising Flour

½ teaspoon baking soda

2 large eggs, separated

5⅓ tablespoons (⅓ cup) butter, melted

1 cup buttermilk

Preheat lightly greased waffle iron.

Combine flour and baking soda. Combine egg yolks, butter, and milk. Stir liquids into flour mixture. Beat egg whites until stiff. Fold in egg whites.

Pour ½ cup of batter in center of the lower half of the waffle iron. Cook waffles until no steam shows around the edges. Lift top and gently loosen waffle with a fork. Remove waffle and serve at once.

Makes five 7½-inch round waffles.

Variations

Pecan Waffles Drizzled with Nutmeg and Honey: Sprinkle 2 tablespoons pecans over waffle batter after pouring in waffle iron. Dust waffles with nutmeg if desired. Serve with honey.

Berry Yogurt Waffles: Top waffles with yogurt, fresh strawberries, and blueberries. For a dessert waffle, try frozen strawberry yogurt and banana slices.

Circa 1940

Southern Grits Waffles

*A recipe contest held by White Lily more than 50 years ago
paid this winner the $1 grand prize.*

And from the "Marshes of Glynn" Mrs. Edgar Langston, 1515 Egmont Street,
Brunswick, Ga., shares with us this recipe discovered by her mother.

1 cup cold grits (left-over)

1 cup flour, sifted

3½ teaspoons baking powder

2 teaspoons Georgia cane syrup

2 eggs

1½ cup milk

5 tablespoons butter or margarine

Beat the eggs, add milk, syrup, grits and flour (to which baking powder has been added)
beating until smooth. Add shortening last of all and mix all well.

Note: The addition of syrup gives the waffles a delicious flavor and a golden brown color.

Cornmeal Waffles

This same recipe was named Corn Pone Waffles in the 1932 White Lily flour cookbook. Waffles aren't served just at breakfast in the South. Although these are good with syrup, they are equally delicious any time of day. They are like corn bread, of course, but crisper. Pour molasses over them for breakfast, or top with chili for a quick, hot supper.

1½ cups White Lily Self-Rising Cornmeal Mix

½ cup White Lily Self-Rising Flour

1 tablespoon sugar

1 large egg, lightly beaten

1½ cups milk

4 tablespoons butter, melted

Preheat lightly greased waffle iron.

Combine cornmeal mix, flour, and sugar in medium bowl. In another bowl, combine egg, milk, and butter. Stir into flour mixture.

Pour ½ cup of batter in center of the lower half of the waffle iron. Cook waffles until no steam shows around the edges. Lift top and gently loosen waffle with a fork. Remove waffle and serve at once.

Makes six 7½-inch round waffles.

Circa 1930

Johnny Cake

The name Johnny Cake may come from joniken, a Native American word for flat cornmeal cakes. The early settlers called them Indian cakes. Cakes made of cornmeal and water and cooked by field workers on the blade of a hoe were called hoe cakes. This recipe is straight from the 1930s White Lily cookbook, but these days, you can use 2¼ cups of White Lily Cornmeal Mix to replace the first five ingredients.

1¼ cups sifted White Lily Flour

¾ teaspoon soda

2 teaspoons baking powder

1 teaspoon salt

1 cup cornmeal

2 tablespoons sugar

2 well-beaten eggs

1 cup sour milk or buttermilk

3 tablespoons melted fat

Sift together flour, soda, baking powder, salt, cornmeal, and sugar. Combine beaten eggs, milk, and fat. Pour into flour-meal mixture all at once. Stir only enough to mix. Pour into shallow, oiled pan. Bake in hot oven (425° F) about 40 minutes.

Yield: 1 sheet, about 8x8x1-inch.

Yeast Breads

The joy of baking bread is one of life's simple pleasures. It takes time, but it's relaxing, fulfilling, and wholly satisfying. The yeast gives off an earthy fragrance as it works its magic. The dough springs back as you knead it with your hands. And the flour, yeast, and other ingredients coming together in your kitchen seems a miracle. That's why bread-making remains a timeless art.

The South may be known for its biscuits, but special occasions, such as a long-awaited homecoming or a formal dinner, seem to call for fancy yeast breads. The warm, welcoming smell of baking yeast bread-makes guests feel comfortable and cozy.

Because yeast bread seems the very symbol of warmth, it is often baked to ward off the chill of cold, dreary winter months. And since there is little more soothing than the smell of baking bread, cooks everywhere favor it for making someone who's had a hard day feel just a little bit better.

Baking yeast bread hasn't always been as easy as it is today. It was at least a two-day process. The day before the actual bread-making began, the cook would "set a sponge" – a special combination of flour, milk and sugar designed to attract a fine-flavored and lively wild yeast. The next morning the bread would be mixed, allowed to rise one or more times, kneaded, and baked. Scrapings in the bowl were carefully saved for the next bread-baking session.

When reliable yeast became available, cooks concocted a new creation – a soft, fluffy yeast roll with none of the crustiness of European-style hard rolls. These soft, buttery rolls broke the traditional rules of bread-making by using soft wheat flour, because that was the type grown in the Southern states, instead of the hard wheat bread flour that was available in the Northern states. These delicious rolls were refined even more with the arrival of refrigerators. They could be refrigerated, shaped, and baked later, making hot rolls possible with only a couple hours' notice.

Homemade bread of any sort is a rare delight these days. If you want to treat your guests, family, or friends to something extra special, bake up a little extra love and care with some fresh, steaming yeast rolls or hot cross buns with lemon glaze. And reward yourself with some simple stress relief at the same time.

Breads and rolls freeze well, too. On a rainy day, getting the kids involved with fixing rolls can be fun. Then freeze them, and you'll have homemade bread ready for special-occasion meals.

Sally Lunn Bread

This light sweet bread appeared in several cookbooks written by Mrs. Elizabeth Stanfield for White Lily. Sally Lunn is said to have been a baker in Bath, England, but the bread's name could be derived from the French words for sun and moon – soleil and lune.

1 package active dry yeast

¼ cup warm water (105° F to 115° F)

½ cup sugar

2 tablespoons vegetable shortening

2 eggs

1 teaspoon salt

3¾ cups White Lily Bread Flour

1 cup warm milk (105° F to 115° F)

Soften yeast in warm water. Set aside. In mixer bowl, cream together sugar and shortening. Beat in eggs and salt. Stir in 1½ cups flour and beat for 3 minutes on high speed. Stir in milk and softened yeast. Mix well. Add remaining flour and beat for 1 minute on high speed. Cover bowl. Let dough rise in warm place until doubled in size (about 1 hour).

Grease a 10-inch fluted tube pan. Stir down batter and spoon evenly into prepared pan. Cover and let rise again until doubled in size (30 to 45 minutes). Preheat oven to 325° F. Bake for 10 minutes. Increase oven temperature to 375° F. Continue baking for 20 minutes. Remove bread from pan to wire rack. Serve warm or cool.

Makes one 10-inch loaf.

Feather-Light Dinner Rolls

2 packages active dry yeast

½ cup warm water (105° F to 115° F)

1½ cups milk

½ cup sugar

2 teaspoons salt

¼ cup shortening

1 large egg, lightly beaten

5½ to 6 cups White Lily Bread Flour

Melted butter for brushing tops

In large bowl, dissolve yeast in warm water. In saucepan, heat milk, sugar, salt, and shortening to 115° F. Add to yeast mixture in bowl. Stir in egg. Beat in 3 cups of the flour until dough is fairly smooth. Stir in enough of the remaining flour to make a very soft dough. Turn out onto lightly floured surface. Knead 5 minutes, adding flour by the tablespoon as needed to prevent sticking. Form into a ball. Place in greased bowl, turning so greased surface is on top.

Cover with damp cloth or plastic wrap. Let rise in a warm place until doubled in size, about 1½ hours.

Preheat oven to 400° F. Grease two 13 x 9 x 2-inch pans.

Punch down dough. Turn onto lightly floured surface. Divide dough into 30 equal pieces. Shape into balls. Place balls on greased pans. Cover with damp cloth and let rise in a warm place until doubled in size, about 20 minutes.

Bake for 15 to 20 minutes, or until golden brown. Brush tops with butter. Serve hot out of the oven or cool.

Makes 30 rolls.

Note: For more flavor, dough may be refrigerated after first rising for up to 3 days, then shaped into rolls. Allow to rise until doubled (about one hour) and bake as directed.

Flaky Potato Rolls

In yeast breads, potato joins flour for a balance of flavor and smooth texture.

2 medium potatoes, peeled and quartered

1 cup milk

1 package active dry yeast

½ cup sugar

⅔ cup vegetable oil

1 large egg, lightly beaten

2 teaspoons salt

6 to 6½ cups White Lily Bread Flour

Melted butter for brushing tops

Cook potatoes in boiling water until tender, about 20 minutes. Drain potatoes, reserving ½ cup of potato water. Combine potato water and milk and heat until warm (105° F to 115° F). Stir in yeast and sugar. Let stand until dissolved.

Mash potatoes. Combine 1 cup of mashed potatoes, oil, egg, salt, and yeast mixture. Blend well. Add flour until stiff dough is formed. Turn out onto lightly floured surface. Knead for 8 to 10 minutes, adding flour as needed to prevent sticking. Place in greased bowl, turning dough so greased surface is on top.

Cover with damp cloth or plastic wrap and let rise in warm place until doubled in size, about 1½ hours.

Preheat oven to 400° F. Grease four 9-inch round cake pans.

Punch down dough. Divide in fourths. Divide each fourth into twelve 1½-inch balls. Place in prepared pans. Cover with damp cloth or plastic wrap. Let rise in a warm place until doubled in size, about 45 minutes.

Bake for 12 to 15 minutes, or until golden brown. Brush tops with melted butter. Remove to wire rack to cool. Serve warm.

Makes 4 dozen small rolls.

TIPS FOR MAKING YEAST BREADS

Be sure to choose the right flour for the type of bread you're making. For yeast breads, high protein flour is best. When kneaded, the proteins blend with liquids to form gluten. As yeast generates gases, gluten acts like little balloons, lifting the dough so the bread rises high and light. Without these gluten "balloons," the yeast bread does not rise. White Lily Bread Flour was made to work just right. (Plain All-Purpose Flour simply does not have enough protein to sustain yeast breads.)

MASTERING DOUGH

Dough can be kneaded in a food processor or electric stand mixer with a dough hook. However, many people enjoy the stress relief of kneading by hand.

To determine whether the dough has been kneaded enough, pinch off a small piece of dough, flatten it, and stretch it out. The dough should stretch so it is thin enough to see through. If it immediately breaks, continue kneading.

Finding a warm place for the dough to rise can be difficult in an air-conditioned kitchen. The best temperature is 80° F to 90° F. Any warm place, such as the top of your refrigerator or dryer, will work. Many cooks place a pan of boiling water on the bottom rack of the oven and put the covered dough above.

Allowing bread to rise long enough is very important. It should double in size. Press lightly with your finger to tell if the dough is ready. The indention should remain on the surface. If it does, the dough is ready to be punched down to remove pockets of yeast. If these bubbles are allowed to remain, your bread will have large air pockets.

Now you're ready to shape the dough according to instructions in the recipe. If the dough springs back, cover it and allow it to rest for a few minutes.

TIPS FOR MAKING YEAST BREADS

BAKING

To check if bread is done, remove from pan and tap bottom of loaf. It should make a hollow sound. It will read 200° F when tested by an instant thermometer. Remove from the pan and cool on a wire rack.

STORAGE

Bread can be frozen whole or sliced. Packed in freezer bags or wrapped in heavy-duty aluminum foil, it freezes very well. It can later be thawed at room temperature or heated in the oven, toaster, or toaster oven at 350° F until thawed. *Never put bread in a refrigerator.* Refrigeration actually causes bread to stale more quickly than room temperature.

Be sure bread is completely cooled before covering with plastic wrap.

Homemade bread will only last a few days at room temperature. The bread you buy at the store contains additives that keep it fresh. However, homemade bread tastes at least ten times better.

Homemade Light Loaf Bread

A loaf of homemade bread on the dinner table will make any cook proud. Don't forget to use leftover slices for gourmet sandwiches and toast. Milk gives these loaves a richer flavor than standard bread.

1 package active dry yeast

½ cup warm water (105° F to 115° F)

1¾ cups milk

2 tablespoons sugar

2 teaspoons salt

2 tablespoons shortening

5¾ to 6¼ cups White Lily Bread Flour

Dissolve yeast in warm water in large bowl. Set aside. In saucepan, heat milk, sugar, salt, and shortening to 115° F. Stir into yeast mixture. Beat in 2½ cups of the flour. Stir in enough of the remaining flour to make a fairly stiff dough.

Turn out onto lightly floured surface. Knead 10 minutes, slowly adding flour a tablespoon at a time as needed to prevent sticking. Place dough in greased bowl, turning so greased surface is on top. Cover with damp cloth or plastic wrap and let rise in a warm place until doubled in size, about 1 hour.

Grease two 8½ x 4½ x 2½-inch loaf pans.

Punch down dough. Turn out onto lightly floured surface. Divide dough in half. Shape each half into smooth ball. Cover with damp towel or plastic wrap. Let rest for 10 minutes. Flatten to remove air bubbles. Roll dough into two 14 x 8-inch rectangles. Roll up tightly (jelly-roll fashion) from short side. Seal seam and ends. Place in greased loaf pans. Cover with damp towel or plastic wrap. Let rise in warm place until double in size, 45 to 60 minutes.

Bake in oven preheated to 375° F for 45 minutes, or until when bread is removed from pan, it sounds hollow when lightly tapped on the bottom. Cover with foil during the last 15 minutes of baking. Remove loaves from pans. Cool on wire racks.

Makes 2 loaves.

Circa 1930

Ice Box Dough for Rolls

This very old White Lily recipe is our most requested recipe for rolls. It breaks the rules by using soft wheat flour rather than the hard wheat bread flour. The result is a soft and light, buttery roll that has graced Southern tables for centuries.

1 package active dry yeast	¼ cup sugar
1½ cups water, divided	1 teaspoon salt
5 cups White Lily Plain All-Purpose Flour	8 tablespoons (1 stick) butter

Dissolve yeast in ½ cup warm water (105° F to 115° F). In large bowl, combine flour, sugar, and salt.

Divide the butter into pieces and scatter on top of the flour. Work the pieces into the flour with a pastry cutter, two knives, or your fingertips until they are about the size of a pea.

Add dissolved yeast and 1 cup of cool water. Stir several minutes until stiff dough forms. Place in another large, greased bowl. Cover tightly and place on ice [refrigerate] until ready to use (up to 5 days).

About two hours before baking, remove the dough from refrigerator. Turn out onto lightly floured surface and roll out ½-inch thick. Cut with a 2-inch biscuit cutter. Shape each piece into a ball and place on greased baking sheet. Cover with a damp towel and let rise in a warm place until doubled in size. This may take as long as 1½ hours.

Preheat oven to 450° F. Bake for 15 minutes, or until light golden brown. Brush tops with butter. Serve hot out of the oven.

Makes 2 dozen rolls.

Hot Cross Buns with Lemon Glaze

Hot Cross Buns are traditionally served on Good Friday, but of course they are good anytime, especially as a light, sweet breakfast roll or dessert. These are made by cutting a cross in each bun's top, which is filled with a lemon glaze after baking.

2 packages active dry yeast

¼ cup warm water (105° F to 115° F)

¾ cup milk

8 tablespoons (1 stick) butter

⅓ cup sugar

¾ teaspoon salt

3 large eggs

5 to 5½ cups White Lily Bread Flour

¾ teaspoon ground cinnamon

¼ teaspoon ground cloves

¼ teaspoon ground nutmeg

¾ cup raisins

2 teaspoons orange zest

1 large egg yolk

1 teaspoon water

Lemon Glaze

1 cup confectioners' sugar

1 tablespoon milk

½ teaspoon lemon extract

Dissolve yeast in warm water in large bowl. Set aside. In saucepan, bring milk to just below boiling point and stir in butter. Cool to lukewarm. Add sugar and salt to milk mixture. In bowl, blend yeast mixture, milk mixture, and eggs. Combine 4½ cups of the flour, the cinnamon, cloves, nutmeg, raisins, and orange zest. Gradually add flour mixture to liquid and mix well. Turn out onto lightly floured surface. Knead for about 5 minutes, adding flour as necessary to prevent sticking. Place in a greased bowl, turning so greased surface is on top. Cover with damp cloth or plastic wrap. Let rise in warm place until doubled in size, about one hour.

  Punch down dough. Pinch off pieces of dough the size of golf balls and roll into smooth balls. Place on lightly greased baking sheets. Let rise in warm place until doubled in size, about 45 minutes.

  Preheat oven to 375° F. Cut a shallow X, using a sharp knife, in the top of each bun. Mix egg yolk and water and brush mixture on tops of each bun. Bake for 12 to 15 minutes. Cool on wire racks.

Make the glaze by combining confectioners' sugar, milk, and lemon extract and stirring until smooth. Drizzle glaze to fill in the X cut into the top of buns.

Serve warm.

Makes 3 dozen buns.

ABOUT YEAST

Yeast comes in a variety of forms. The one you'll use most is active dry yeast. Make sure it's fresh.

Active dry yeast needs to be dissolved in water that is 105° F to 115° F. Check water temperature with a kitchen thermometer. Hot water kills yeast and water that is too cold will not activate it.

Quick-rising yeast works great and can be mixed directly with the flour, eliminating the dissolving step.

Packages of yeast have use-by dates, but you can also check yeast by adding it and a pinch of sugar to warm water (105° F to 115° F). If small bubbles form, the yeast is working.

Focaccia with Red Peppers and Onions

This bread is perfect served with soups, salads, and grilled meats.

1 package active dry yeast

1 cup warm water (105° F to 115° F)

1 tablespoon sugar

3 to 3½ cups White Lily Bread Flour

1 teaspoon salt

¼ cup plus 2 tablespoons olive oil

½ red bell pepper, thinly sliced

½ medium onion, thinly sliced

1½ teaspoons chopped fresh rosemary

¼ cup coarsely chopped, pitted black olives

½ teaspoon kosher or sea salt

Dissolve yeast in warm water in large bowl. Add sugar. Blend flour and salt. Gradually add to dissolved yeast. Add ¼ cup olive oil.

Turn out onto lightly floured surface and knead for 5 to 10 minutes, adding flour as necessary to prevent sticking. Place in a greased bowl, turning so greased surface is on top. Cover with damp cloth or plastic wrap. Let rise in warm place until doubled in size, about one hour.

Preheat oven to 425° F. Grease baking sheet or two 9-inch cake pans.

Punch down dough. Shape dough into two balls. Roll each ball to approximately 1 inch thick and place on baking sheet, or press dough into cake pans. Cover with damp towel or plastic wrap, and let double in size (about 45 minutes).

Meanwhile, sauté bell pepper and onion in 2 tablespoons olive oil.

After dough is doubled in size, make indentations in surface with fingers. Gently press sautéed bell pepper and onion into each round of dough. Sprinkle with rosemary, olives, and coarse salt.

Bake for 30 minutes, or until brown.

Makes 10 servings.

Cinnamon Rolls

2 packages active dry yeast
½ cup water
½ cup milk
½ cup sugar
1 teaspoon salt
½ cup shortening
2 eggs, lightly beaten
4 to 4½ cups White Lily Bread Flour, divided

Caramel Coating

1 cup butter
1 cup packed brown sugar
1 cup pecans
¼ cup corn syrup, optional

Filling

4 tablespoons butter, softened
1 cup sugar
1 tablespoon plus 1 teaspoon cinnamon

Dissolve yeast in warm water in large bowl. Set aside. Heat milk, sugar, salt, and shortening to 105° F to 115° F. Stir milk mixture and eggs into yeast mixture. Beat in 2 cups flour. Stir in enough of remaining flour to make a soft dough.

Turn onto lightly floured surface. Knead 5 minutes, adding 1 tablespoon flour at a time, as needed, to prevent sticking. Form into ball. Place in greased bowl, turning to grease surface of dough. Cover with damp cloth. Let rise in a warm place (such as oven with pan of very hot tap water on rack below) for 1½ hours or until doubled in size. Divide dough in half.

To make the caramel coating, melt ½ cup butter in each of two 13 x 9 x 2-inch pans. In each pan, stir in half of the brown sugar, pecans, and, if desired, corn syrup. Set aside.

Roll dough into two 15 x 13-inch rectangles.

To make the filling, spread each rectangle with 2 tablespoons butter. Mix sugar and cinnamon, and sprinkle half of the mixture evenly over each rectangle.

Roll dough up, jelly-roll fashion, from long side. Seal seam and cut roll into fifteen 1-inch slices. Place slices, cut side down, on top of caramel coating in pan. Cover pans with damp cloth.

Preheat oven to 375° F. Let dough rise in a warm place for 30 minutes or until doubled in size.

Bake for 25 to 30 minutes. Invert pans onto trays lined with wax paper. Leave pans in place for 5 minutes before removing. Serve warm.

Makes 30 rolls.

Main Dishes

Dinner time! Supper time! Those welcome calls signal more than just a good meal of corn-meal-breaded catfish or crispy fried chicken, which was once considered a Sunday luxury. Main meals have also always meant times of fellowship with family and friends.

Of course, Southern entrees are typically delicious, whether they're traditional favorites such as country fried steak, or one of the new Southern favorites such as corn bread salad or corn bread pizza. Still, what dinner is not made better by the company of loved ones? That may be one of the little secrets that makes down-home cooking so marvelously good. Suppers, whether simple or sumptuous, are almost always eaten amidst family or friends with plenty of lively talk and laughter.

For years, farm families spent their days growing and preparing food. Although the work was satisfying and sustaining, it was also very strenuous. Sitting down together at the midday meal gave people a much-needed rest before they returned to afternoon work in the fields or around the farm. With work mostly done for the day, supper became a time of sharing – when children learned important life lessons through the telling and retelling of stories from the family's past.

Nowadays, most of us find it can be quite a trick just to find time to prepare dinner, much less have the family sit down and eat together. However, in this age of juggled duties and hectic schedules, family time together is more important than ever. In order to live in a world with ever-shifting priorities, it's essential to know who you are, where you came from, and what you believe in. That's an important gift to pass on to your children and grandchildren. What better place or time than at the dinner table?

Cornmeal-Breaded Catfish

Have you noticed that catfish are jumping onto menus everywhere? Catfish was largely ignored until farm-raising began. Farm-raised catfish are grain-fed, resulting in better-tasting catfish with a mellower flavor. Don't forget the hush puppies at your fish fry!

4 (8 to 10 ounce) catfish fillets

½ teaspoon freshly ground black pepper

1½ cups White Lily Self-Rising Cornmeal Mix

Vegetable oil for frying

1 lemon, sliced

In a large, heavy skillet, heat about ¾ inch vegetable oil to 375° F.

Wash catfish in ice water and drain. (This helps breading adhere to fish.)

Sprinkle pepper onto all sides of catfish fillets. Pour cornmeal mix in shallow pan like a cake or pie pan. Place fish into cornmeal. Press lightly to coat. Continue until all fish is breaded.

Place 2 fillets at a time in skillet. Fry on each side for 4 minutes, or until fish is flaky and golden brown. Remove and drain on paper towels. If desired, keep the cooked fillets warm by placing them on a baking sheet in a 200° F oven until ready to serve. Serve fish with a side of crispy Hush Puppies (see page 39).

Makes 4 servings.

Buttermilk-Battered Chicken Breast Fillets

Chicken hasn't always been cheap. Before World War II, a fried chicken dinner was a special Sunday treat. Today, boneless breasts make this Southern favorite quick and easy. Try to use fresh chicken breasts instead of frozen. Some stores get their chicken in from the suppliers already frozen, so check with the butcher. Slice these and serve with salad greens and honey mustard.

4 large boneless, skinless chicken breasts

1½ cups White Lily Plain All-Purpose Flour

1½ teaspoons salt

2 teaspoons freshly ground black pepper

2 large eggs, lightly beaten

1 cup buttermilk

Vegetable oil, or vegetable oil and bacon drippings

In a large, heavy skillet, heat 1½ inches of oil to 365° F.

You will need three bowls to bread the chicken. Thoroughly blend flour, salt, and pepper in a medium bowl. Break eggs into a small bowl, beat slightly, and set aside. Pour buttermilk into a bowl.

Dip chicken breasts, one at a time, into buttermilk, then coat completely with flour mixture. Next, dip chicken breast into beaten eggs. Then dip back into flour. Repeat for other pieces.

Gently place chicken breasts into hot oil. Fry uncovered 10 minutes on each side, or until golden brown and the juices from the chicken no longer run pink.

Drain on paper towels. Serve immediately, or place on pan in a 200° F oven until ready to serve.

Makes 2 to 4 servings.

Circa 1900

Hamburg Pies

This recipe appears in White Lily's earliest cookbook. At the turn of the twentieth century, hamburg referred to tenderized beef, or pounded steak, and sometimes ground beef. By 1912, the beef was served on a bun and called a hamburger. This recipe was pre-bun days and is a nice twist on the burger we know now.

Season one pound of hamburg steak with salt, pepper, and a little prepared mustard and onion juice. Shape into round cakes and wrap in pastry which has been rolled as for pie crust. Brush over with milk and bake in hot oven.

Southern Fried Chicken

Picnics and covered-dish suppers at church must include fried chicken. Using a heavy skillet is important because the oil heats more evenly. For chicken that is tender and absorbs less oil, soak it in salt water (about two tablespoons salt in two quarts water) in the refrigerator for eight hours.

Vegetable oil for frying, or vegetable oil and bacon drippings

1 cup White Lily Plain All-Purpose Flour

½ teaspoon freshly ground black pepper

½ teaspoon salt

1 broiler-fryer (2 to 3 pounds), cut into pieces

½ cup buttermilk

In a heavy iron skillet or electric skillet, preheat about 1½ inches of vegetable oil to 350° F.

Combine flour, pepper, and salt. Dip chicken pieces in buttermilk, then place chicken pieces in flour mixture and toss to coat evenly.

Arrange chicken in skillet so that the pieces are not crowded. Fry 20 to 30 minutes, turning once, or until browned and juices run clear when cut.

Makes 2 to 4 servings.

Variations

Pecan Fried Chicken: **Add ½ cup finely chopped pecans to flour mixture.**

Seasoned Fried Chicken: **Add 2 teaspoons freshly ground black pepper (instead of ½ teaspoon), 1½ teaspoons sage, 1 teaspoon garlic powder, ½ teaspoon cayenne pepper, and ½ teaspoon paprika to flour mixture.**

Country Fried Steak with Gravy

Some areas of the country call this beef entree chicken–fried steak. The meat can be tenderized by pounding or can be purchased already tenderized. Chill steak on ice for one minute before breading to help crust stay on better.

⅓ cup vegetable oil

1⅓ cups White Lily Plain All-Purpose Flour

1 teaspoon salt

⅛ teaspoon garlic powder

3 large eggs

1 cup milk

4 cubed beef steaks

Gravy

¼ cup vegetable oil

¼ cup White Lily Plain All-Purpose Flour

3½ cups milk

1 teaspoon salt

¼ teaspoon freshly ground black pepper

In a large, heavy skillet, heat oil to 350° F. Blend flour, salt, and garlic powder in a medium bowl. Break eggs into small bowl. Add milk to eggs and beat slightly. Dip steaks in egg mixture, then coat with flour mixture. Place steaks in hot oil. Fry 6 to 8 minutes on each side. Remove steaks from oil and drain on paper towels.

To make Gravy, add oil to the skillet with the beef steak drippings. Stir in the flour and blend well. Add milk and stir over medium heat until gravy begins to boil. Reduce heat to low. Add salt and pepper.

Return steaks to gravy. Cover and simmer 40 minutes, stirring occasionally. Spoon gravy over steaks before serving.

Makes 4 servings.

Circa 1940

Beef in Cream Sauce for Short Cake Luncheon

Shortcake usually brings images of fresh fruit and whipped cream — dessert.
However, Southerners over the centuries have topped biscuits with
creamed chicken or beef. This recipe was in the
1940 White Lily cookbook.

1 Cup cream sauce
2 Cup cold cooked beef run through food chopper or finely minced

Rich biscuit dough cut in large circles, baked quickly in hot oven, then split, and toasted.
  Fill toasted biscuit with the creamed meat. Serve at once, with green vegetable salad, a cookie and a drink.

Chicken and Dumplings with Vegetables

The flat Southern dumpling is basically biscuit dough rolled out to about ¼ inch thick, cut in strips with a pizza cutter or knife, and cooked in rich chicken broth. This dish was popular in the past because with good dumplings only a few bits of chicken made a meal. Today, it's just popular. We added vegetables to this recipe to make it a healthy, one-pot meal, but they can be omitted for the more traditional dish.

1 (3 to 4 pound) chicken, cut into pieces

1 medium onion, quartered

2 bay leaves

4 carrots, sliced into 1-inch pieces

1 medium onion, chopped into 1-inch pieces

2 celery stalks, sliced into 1-inch pieces

2 cups White Lily Self-Rising Flour

¼ cup vegetable shortening

¾ cup milk or buttermilk

4 tablespoons butter or chicken fat

¼ cup White Lily Plain All-Purpose Flour

1 teaspoon salt

½ teaspoon freshly ground black pepper

¼ cup half-and-half, optional

Add chicken, quartered onion, and bay leaves to Dutch oven or large stock pot. Cover with 6 cups of water. Bring to a boil, reduce heat to low, and cover. Cook 30 minutes, or until chicken is done. Remove the chicken from the pot. As soon as chicken is cool enough to handle, remove meat from bones, cut into 1-inch pieces, and place in refrigerator until ready to use. Return skin and bones to liquid and cook as long as time permits, up to 4 hours. Strain the broth and reserve in a bowl.

Steam carrots, chopped onion, and celery for 10 minutes or until just tender. Set aside.

To prepare the dumplings, measure self-rising flour into a bowl. Cut in shortening using a pastry blender, two knives, or your fingertips until mixture resembles coarse crumbs. Stir in buttermilk or milk until well blended. Roll dough on a lightly floured surface until it is about ¼ inch thick. Slice into 2 x ½-inch strips.

In the Dutch oven, melt 4 tablespoons of either butter or chicken fat from the surface of the reserved broth. Blend with ¼ cup all-purpose flour. Heat, stirring constantly, for 1 minute. Add 4 cups of chicken broth. Add salt and pepper and, if desired, half-and-half. Bring to a boil. (If you'd like, freeze the additional chicken broth for other uses.)

Add chicken and vegetables to broth. Return to boil. Then add prepared dumplings to broth. Cover and boil 15 minutes, or until dumplings are firm.

Serve immediately in soup bowls.

Makes 6 servings.

Hearty Beef Stew with Herbed Dumplings

1 tablespoon vegetable oil

6 ounces boneless beef, cut into 2-inch pieces

6 cups beef broth

1 medium onion, chopped

1 large potato, peeled and cubed

4 carrots, peeled and sliced

1 celery stalk

½ teaspoon salt

¼ teaspoon freshly ground black pepper

Herbed Dumplings

1 large egg

½ cup milk

1¼ cups White Lily Self-Rising Flour

1 tablespoon dried parsley

½ teaspoon dried thyme

In a Dutch oven, heat vegetable oil until sizzling. Add the beef and brown on all sides. Drain. Add beef broth, vegetables, salt, and pepper. Simmer 20 to 30 minutes.

To make the Herbed Dumplings, beat egg and milk together. Mix flour, parsley, and thyme. Add egg-milk mixture to flour mixture and stir to make a stiff dough.

Drop dumpling batter by tablespoons into simmering stew. Cover and simmer 10 minutes. Dumplings are done when they float on top of the liquid.

Makes 6 servings.

Circa 1930

Chicken and Ham Timbales

Dishes similar to this 1930s White Lily recipe are showing up at fine restaurants these days.

1 Tablespoon finely chopped parsley	1¾ cup thick cream sauce
1 cup minced cooked chicken	1 egg yolk
½ cup minced cooked ham	salt and pepper

Oil custard cups, sprinkle with finely chopped parsley. Fill cups with creamed chicken mixture. Place cups in pan of water, cover and bake about 30 minutes. Garnish with thin cream sauce, chopped green peppers and onions that have been cooked in 2 Tablespoons shortening until tender.

Vegetable Chili Corn Bread Pie

1 cup diced onion, divided

2 teaspoons vegetable oil, divided

2 cans pinto beans or kidney beans, drained

1 (8 ounce) can tomato sauce

1 (14 ounce) can cut tomatoes, drained

1 package chili seasoning mix

1½ cups White Lily Self-Rising Cornmeal Mix

1 large egg

½ cup salsa

½ cup milk

1 cup shredded cheddar cheese

Preheat oven to 425° F. Lightly grease a 2-quart casserole dish.

In a stockpot or Dutch oven, sauté ½ cup of the onion in 1 teaspoon vegetable oil until tender. Add beans, tomato sauce, tomatoes, and chili seasoning mix. Bring to a boil, reduce heat and simmer 5 minutes, or until thickened.

In a mixing bowl, prepare topping by blending cornmeal mix, remaining vegetable oil, egg, salsa, milk, and the remaining diced onion.

Spread half of the corn bread mixture in prepared dish. Pour in all of the chili mixture. Spread the remaining corn bread mixture on top.

Bake for 25 to 30 minutes, or until corn bread is golden brown. Top with cheese and return to oven for 5 minutes, or until cheese is melted.

Makes 6 to 8 servings.

Chicken Pot Pie

This recipe features two easy toppings: a biscuit crust or a pie crust. Choose your favorite for a one-dish meal that includes plenty of vegetables.

1½ cups cooked chicken cut into 2-inch pieces

3 cups homemade chicken broth or 2 (14-ounce) cans unsalted chicken broth

4 carrots, sliced into ½-inch pieces

2 medium onions, finely chopped

3 celery stalks, sliced into ½-inch pieces

4 tablespoons butter

4 tablespoons White Lily Plain All-Purpose Flour

¼ cup heavy cream

1 teaspoon salt

½ teaspoon freshly ground black pepper

1 cup frozen peas

Pie Crust Topping

1½ cups White Lily Plain All-Purpose Flour

1 teaspoon salt

3 tablespoons shortening

3 tablespoons butter

6 to 8 tablespoons ice-cold water or milk

1 egg, lightly beaten

Biscuit Crust Topping

2 cups White Lily Self-Rising Flour

¼ cup shortening

¾ cup milk or buttermilk

Make Pie Crust Topping if desired. Combine flour and salt in large bowl. Blend the shortening and butter into the flour using a pastry cutter, two knives, or your fingertips. Sprinkle several tablespoons ice-cold water or milk over part of mixture. Toss gently with fork and push to side of bowl. Repeat just until the mixture is moistened and you can form it into a ball. Flatten ball of dough into a disk. Wrap tightly with plastic wrap and refrigerate dough for 30 minutes to overnight.

Cook chicken and broth in a large stock pot as directed in recipe for Chicken and Dumplings with Vegetables (see page 86), or use frozen cooked chicken and canned broth.

Steam carrots, onions, and celery for 10 minutes, or until just tender. Remove from steamer and set aside.

Preheat oven to 400° F.

Melt butter in saucepan over medium heat. Stir in flour; heat 1 minute. Gradually add heavy cream, chicken broth, salt, and pepper. Heat until thickened. Stir in steamed vegetables, frozen peas, and chicken. Pour into a 9 x 13-inch pan or individual dishes.

If you are using the Pie Crust Topping, remove disk of dough from the refrigerator. If necessary, allow to sit for 5 minutes to soften. Gently roll the dough out on a lightly floured surface, place over filling, and brush with beaten egg. Bake for 35 to 40 minutes, or until crust is golden brown.

To make Biscuit Crust Topping, measure flour into bowl. Work the shortening into the flour using a pastry cutter, two knives, or your fingertips until the pieces are about the size of peas. Add milk; mix just until all the flour is moistened. Roll on lightly floured surface to ½ inch thick. Cut using 2-inch cutter. Place biscuits on top of filling. Bake at 400° F for 30 minutes, or until biscuits are lightly browned.

Makes 6 servings.

"DO YOU HAVE ANYTHING TO DECLARE?"

If you live outside the South, White Lily Flour can be a little hard to come by. Desperate for some White Lily Flour, one couple went so far as to carry an empty suitcase with them on their trip down south to make sure they'd have room to pack a few bags of White Lily to take back home. A bit of bad luck caught up with them at bag check-in. The overstuffed suitcase popped open, the White Lily bag broke, and flour flew everywhere. Afraid of being detained for transporting something much more serious than flour, the couple was happily relieved when the bag checker told a fellow worker, "Just more people taking home White Lily Flour."

Barbecued Chicken Corn Bread Pizza

A corn bread pizza crust topped with barbecued chicken is a new twist on old Southern favorites. The corn bread crust is so good that you will want to create other pizzas using this unique crust.

1 pound boneless, skinless chicken breasts

2 cups barbecue sauce, divided

2¼ teaspoons (one package) yeast

1½ cups warm water (105° F to 115° F)

2 cups White Lily Self-Rising Cornmeal Mix

1 teaspoon salt

2 teaspoons sugar

2 cups White Lily Bread Flour

1 tablespoon olive oil

1 medium red onion, diced

1 medium red pepper, diced

1 cup sliced mushrooms

2 cups shredded provolone or mozzarella cheese

Marinate chicken breasts in refrigerator in 1 cup of barbecue sauce for at least 30 minutes.

In a large mixing bowl, dissolve yeast in warm water. Add cornmeal mix, salt, and sugar and mix well. Gradually add flour until the dough pulls away from the side of the bowl and is soft.

Flour your hands and turn dough onto lightly floured surface. Knead by turning and folding for 10 minutes or pulse in food processor or electric mixer. Grease a medium bowl with olive oil. Place dough into bowl and turn once to coat with oil. Cover bowl with plastic wrap and allow to rise in warm place until doubled in size, about 1 hour. Punch down the dough. Dough may be used immediately or wrapped in plastic wrap and refrigerated for up to 24 hours.

If using refrigerated dough, allow dough to sit at room temperature to warm for 30 minutes before rolling.

Preheat oven to 450° F. Lightly grease two pizza pans or baking sheets with olive oil or nonstick cooking spray. Divide dough in half, and make into two balls. Sprinkle pan surfaces with flour or cornmeal. Roll dough to fit and place on prepared pans. Let the dough rise in the pans about 15 minutes. Bake for 12 to 20 minutes or until crust is golden brown.

To prepare the chicken, preheat oven to 350° F. Place breasts in single layer in shallow baking dish. Cover with foil. Bake until done, about 20 minutes. Cut chicken into ¼- to ½-inch pieces.

Spread ½ cup of remaining barbecue sauce on each pizza crust. Top with chicken and vegetables. Bake for 15 minutes. Remove from oven and top each pizza with 1 cup of shredded cheese. Return to oven and bake for 5 minutes, or until cheese is melted.

Makes two 12-inch pizzas.

Circa 1950

Quickie Dixie Chili

With the 1950s, we entered the "prepared food" era. The White Lily cookbook from that decade included this quick dinner. It's a great way to serve leftover chili.

Filling
2 15-oz. Cans prepared chili
1 6-oz. Can tomato paste
1 Tbsp. Cumin powder
1 Tbsp. Chili powder

Corn Meal Biscuit
¾ cup sifted WHITE LILY Self-rising flour
¾ cup self-rising corn meal
¼ cup oil
⅓ to ½ cup milk

Combine chili, tomato paste, cumin, and chili powder in saucepan. Heat to bubbling and simmer 10 minutes. Pour into 8-inch square pan. Add oil and milk to dry ingredients and mix lightly until dry ingredients are moistened. Add remaining milk if needed to make a stiff batter. With spoon, drop 6 mounds of batter over chili mixture. Bake in 425° F oven 20 to 25 minutes.

Makes 6 servings.

Homemade Hot Tamales

These Southern-style tamales can be prepared ahead of time and frozen, still wrapped, for an easy appetizer or meal. Reheat by boiling or steaming for 15 minutes. This is a "most requested" White Lily recipe.

1 pound ground beef

1 medium onion, chopped

4¼ cups White Lily Self-Rising Cornmeal Mix, divided

2½ tablespoons chili powder, divided

2½ teaspoons salt, divided

¼ teaspoon freshly ground black pepper

¼ teaspoon garlic powder

1 to 2 jalapeño peppers, optional

⅔ cup vegetable shortening

1½ to 2 cups boiling water

Tamale papers or corn husks

In a skillet over medium heat, brown ground beef and onion. Remove from heat and stir in ¼ cup of the cornmeal mix, 2 tablespoons chili powder, ½ teaspoon salt, black pepper, garlic powder, and, if desired, jalapeños. Set aside to cool.

Combine remaining cornmeal mix, shortening, remaining salt, and remaining chili powder until thoroughly blended. Stir in just enough boiling water to make a soft dough.

To assemble tamales, soak tamale papers or corn husks in warm water until soft. Spread each paper with 3 tablespoons of cornmeal mixture, making a rectangle about 3½ x 4½ inches. Place 2 tablespoons of cooled meat filling lengthwise down the center of rectangle. Fold up the bottom edge of paper so cornmeal mixture wraps completely around the meat filling. Continue rolling, tucking both sides of paper in to produce a smooth, sealed roll. Tamales may be tied or just folded.

Carefully place tamales, seam side down, in boiling water. Boil, covered, for 45 minutes. Drain. Remove paper wrappers or corn husks unless freezing. Serve covered with chili or Fresh Tomato Salsa.

Makes 1½ to 2 dozen tamales.

Fresh Tomato Salsa

2 tomatoes, peeled and chopped

1 jalapeño pepper, chopped

1 clove garlic, chopped

½ cup chopped onion

½ teaspoon salt

1 tablespoon fresh cilantro

Combine all ingredients and chill.

Corn Bread Salad

Mediterranean cultures have combined breads and vegetables into crisp summer salads for centuries. Now, the recipe is given Southern appeal by using some of the favorite flavors of the South – corn bread, fresh sweet onions, and juicy ripe tomatoes.

1 recipe Salsa Corn Bread (see page 38)

1 cup nonfat or regular sour cream

1 cup nonfat or regular mayonnaise

1 (1 ounce) package ranch salad dressing mix

3 medium tomatoes, diced into ½-inch pieces

1 medium onion, diced into ¼-inch pieces

1 small green pepper, diced into ¼-inch pieces

1 tablespoon minced fresh cilantro or 1 teaspoon dried cilantro

2 (15 ounce) cans pinto beans or black beans, rinsed and drained thoroughly

2 cups shredded low-fat or regular cheddar cheese

Make Salsa Cornbread. Allow to cool completely. Corn bread may be covered with plastic wrap and stored up to forty-eight hours before assembling salad.

In a small bowl, blend sour cream, mayonnaise, and salad dressing mix.

In another bowl, lightly toss together tomatoes, onion, pepper, and cilantro. Drain any juices before assembling salad.

Crumble half of the corn bread into a large serving bowl. Next layer half of the beans, one-third of the tomato mixture, half of the salad dressing, and half of the cheese. Repeat layers. Garnish top with remaining tomato mixture.

Cover and chill for at least two hours and up to twenty-four hours before serving.

Makes 8 servings.

Side Dishes

While main dishes are the heart of the meal, side dishes are the soul. They lend themselves perfectly to the subtle skills cooks have with summer vegetables. From crispy fried okra to light, delicate spoon bread, these are the dishes that disappear first at those famed after-church dinners on the grounds and long-awaited family reunions. And for those folks craving home-cooked country food, nothing satisfies as well as garden-fresh vegetables with piping hot corn bread.

Many people don't realize that creative side dishes were often born of desperation. With meat frequently missing from the table during lean years, cooks turned their imagination and ingenuity to finding new ways to fill empty stomachs.

At certain points, people were so hungry they would fry up anything they could pick or catch. Take fried green tomatoes, for instance. To a hungry man, one extra day was too long to wait for a tomato to ripen to a rich, red glow. So, people picked them green. They found that the tart, tangy taste of the green tomato was complemented nicely by cornmeal, another long-standing Southern staple. A plate of fresh, fried green tomatoes washed down with a cold glass of buttermilk would halt the rumbling in the stomach and provide enough strength to do the work that had to be done.

Today, side dishes still offer the perfect opportunity to show off your versatility with vegetables, a food we're all encouraged to eat more of. The very variety of these dishes — from the trendy tomato aspic to corn bread dressing — will add the perfect touch to any meal, whether you're cooking for just a few or for a crowd.

Fried Okra and Green Tomatoes

This Southern favorite originated in Africa, where the word for okra is "gombo." Choose small okra with a light color. High in vitamins A and C, okra will stay fresh for a week in the refrigerator. If green tomatoes aren't available, select very firm red tomatoes.

½ cup vegetable oil

1 pound fresh okra, cut into ¼-inch slices

1 medium green tomato or firm red tomato, chopped into ½-inch cubes

1 small onion, chopped into ½-inch cubes

¾ cup White Lily Self-Rising Cornmeal Mix

Salt and pepper to taste

In large, heavy skillet, preheat vegetable oil to 350° F. Combine okra, tomato, and onion in medium bowl. Add cornmeal and toss to coat. Place vegetables gently in skillet.

Fry for 3 minutes until cornmeal begins to brown. Turn vegetables gently, and fry for an additional 3 minutes. Reduce heat to medium-low and cook, turning occasionally, until okra is tender, about 5 minutes. Sprinkle on salt and pepper to taste. Serve immediately.

Makes 4 to 6 servings.

Oven–Baked Spicy Vidalia Onion Rings

½ cup White Lily Self-Rising Cornmeal Mix
¼ teaspoon freshly ground black pepper
¼ teaspoon paprika
3 large Vidalia onions sliced into ¼-inch rings
¼ cup milk
2 to 3 tablespoons butter, melted, or nonstick cooking spray
Salt and freshly ground black pepper to taste

Preheat oven to 450° F. Grease baking sheet with nonstick cooking spray. Combine cornmeal mix, pepper, and paprika in large zip-top plastic bag.

Dip onion slices in milk, then place in plastic bag. Seal bag and shake until onion slices are well coated. Place in single layer on pan. Drizzle with melted butter or spray with nonstick cooking spray.

Bake for 10 minutes. Remove from oven and turn onions over with spatula. Return to oven to bake an additional 5 to 10 minutes, or until browned and crisp. Drain on paper towels. Add salt and pepper to taste. Serve while hot.

Makes 4 servings.

Note: You may substitute other vegetables such as green tomatoes, zucchini slices, peeled eggplant slices, or okra. Cut vegetables uniformly in ¼- or ½-inch slices.

Fresh Summer Vegetables in Corn Bread Bowl

A colorful assortment of vegetables served in the center of a ring of corn bread will fill the bill for adding garden vegetables to the table.

2 cups White Lily Self-Rising Cornmeal Mix

1 tablespoon sugar

½ teaspoon sage

½ teaspoon dry mustard

1 cup milk

1 egg, lightly beaten

¼ cup vegetable oil

¼ cup finely chopped onion

¼ cup diced celery

Fresh Summer Vegetables

2 tablespoons butter

1 cup zucchini sliced ¼-inch thick

1 cup yellow squash sliced ¼-inch thick

½ cup sliced fresh mushrooms

½ cup chopped onion

1 clove garlic, minced

½ teaspoon basil

¼ teaspoon oregano

½ teaspoon salt

¼ teaspoon freshly ground black pepper

1 medium tomato, cut into 8 wedges

Preheat oven to 425° F. Grease a 5½-cup oven-proof ring mold.

In a medium bowl, combine cornmeal mix, sugar, sage, and mustard. In another bowl, combine milk, egg, and oil and add to dry ingredients, stirring just until moistened. Stir in onion and celery. Pour into prepared ring mold. Bake for 25 to 30 minutes.

Meanwhile, prepare the vegetables. Heat butter in large skillet over medium-high heat until sizzling. Add all ingredients except tomatoes. Sauté 4 minutes, stirring often. Add tomato wedges and cook 2 minutes, or until heated through.

Turn corn bread out onto a serving plate. Spoon vegetable mixture into a bowl that fits the center of the ring mold and place bowl in corn bread ring.

Makes 6 servings.

Circa 1900

Quick Tomato Aspic

Aspics don't contain a White Lily product, but in the old days, a White Lily cookbook wasn't considered complete without a recipe for this side dish. Use canned tomato juice or soup in place of the tomato sour.

1 tablespoon gelatine soaked in 4 tablespoons cold water, and dissolved over hot water

1 Can of tomato sour
1 Onion minced
1 Green pepper (if desired)

Salt and pepper to taste. Put in well oiled molds, chill. Serve on crisp lettuce.

Stewed Tomatoes with Cornmeal Dumplings

Cornmeal dumplings have long been a Native American dish. This one is simmered with basil and tomatoes. A green vegetable and a meat complete the meal.

4 tablespoons butter

½ cup diced onion

¼ cup diced green bell pepper

1 (28 ounce) can diced or chopped tomatoes, undrained

1 teaspoon brown sugar

½ teaspoon salt

½ teaspoon pepper

1 teaspoon dried basil or 2 tablespoons chopped fresh basil

Cornmeal Dumplings

1 cup White Lily Self-Rising Cornmeal Mix

2 tablespoons shortening

¼ cup shredded cheddar cheese

½ cup milk

Melt butter in skillet over medium heat. Add onion and pepper and sauté for 5 minutes, or until tender. Stir in tomatoes, sugar, salt, pepper, and basil. Bring to a boil.

To prepare dumplings, measure cornmeal into small bowl. Work in the shortening with a pastry blender, two knives, or your fingertips until crumbly. Add cheese and milk. Stir just until moistened.

Drop tablespoons of batter into stewed tomatoes. Cover skillet and simmer 20 minutes, or until dumplings are cooked through.

Makes 4 servings.

Corn Bread–Sausage Dressing

Dressing made with corn bread is the Southern favorite. Most people won't know that sausage is in this dish. They just know it tastes wonderful. This recipe makes a lot of dressing to serve the whole family or stuff in the turkey at Thanksgiving.

1 pound sausage

1 cup chopped onions

2 cups chopped celery

2 (12 ounce) cans cream of chicken soup

1 (14½ ounce) can chicken broth

½ teaspoon salt

3 teaspoons sage

1 teaspoon poultry seasoning

½ teaspoon freshly ground black pepper

2 large eggs, lightly beaten

½ cup hot water

Corn Bread

1 (2 pound) bag White Lily Self-Rising Cornmeal Mix

2 large eggs

⅓ cup vegetable oil

2½ cups milk

To make the cornbread, preheat oven to 425° F. Combine all corn bread ingredients and pour into a greased 13 x 9 x 2-inch pan. Bake 30 minutes, or until golden brown. Cool completely.

To make the dressing, preheat oven to 400° F. Lightly grease a 13 x 9 x 2-inch baking pan and an 8 x 8-inch baking pan.

In a skillet over medium heat, combine sausage, onion, and celery. Cook, stirring often, until sausage is browned and crumbled. Drain thoroughly.

Crumble corn bread into a very large bowl. Add sausage mixture. Stir in cream of chicken soup, chicken broth, salt, sage, poultry seasoning, black pepper, eggs, and hot water. Spoon into greased pans.

Bake for 30 to 35 minutes, or until golden brown.

Makes 16 to 20 servings.

Creamy Corn Spoon Bread

Spoon bread is a cross between grits and a soufflé. Using self-rising cornmeal makes this an easy dish to prepare.

1 cup White Lily Self-Rising Cornmeal Mix

1½ cups milk

1 (8¾ ounce) can cream-style corn

4 tablespoons butter or margarine, softened

1 tablespoon sugar

3 large eggs, separated

Preheat oven to 325° F. Grease 2-quart casserole dish.

In large saucepan, combine cornmeal mix and milk. Cook over medium-high heat, stirring constantly, until mixture is very thick. Remove from heat and stir in corn, butter or margarine, sugar, and egg yolks.

Beat egg whites until stiff. Carefully fold egg whites into cornmeal mixture. Pour into prepared dish.

Bake for 55 to 65 minutes, or until knife inserted comes out clean. Serve immediately with butter or margarine. Spoon bread will settle upon standing.

Makes 6 servings.

Circa 1932

Stuffed Artichokes

We selected this unique recipe from the 1932 cookbook.

Remove a few outer tough petals, trim stem even with the base of petals, and cut across top about an inch. Pack upside down in kettle, pour boiling water over them to cover. Cover with plate to weight down under water. Cook for 30 minutes. Remove from water, drain well. Remove the choke, and fill space with a cheese or cooked meat stuffing. Serve with Celery Dressing.

Celery Dressing

1 Cup Mayonnaise	2 Teaspoons lemon juice
1 Cup finely minced celery	1 Teaspoon onion juice, or
2 Tablespoons minced green pepper	2 Tablespoons minced onion
2 Tablespoons minced cucumber	Salt and pepper to taste

Mix in order given.

Cakes

Celebrations call for cake. What birthday is complete without a cake topped with bright candles? Your favorite may be red velvet cake liberally coated with cream cheese frosting or a melt-in-your-mouth black walnut cream cake. And what sweeter or more gracious way to welcome guests into your home than with a fresh-from-the-oven pound cake? There simply is no better way to celebrate than with a cake.

If you take a cake to the church supper, everyone will want the recipe. Fortunately, when cookbooks became available decades ago, it was not uncommon to find half the recipes or more dedicated to satisfying the famed Southern sweet tooth.

Before the invention of baking powder, the traditional pound cake remained at the heart of Southern desserts. Old-fashioned pound cakes contained no leavening, only a pound each of butter, sugar, eggs, and flour, and just a dab of the cook's favorite flavoring. To make the cake rise, the batter was beaten long and hard, often for an hour or more.

But it was the arrival of a reliable form of baking powder that actually sent cooks into a creative cake-baking craze. With a foolproof method for making cakes rise, cooks had more energy and enthusiasm for experimenting. From angel food cake to Lane cake, their new concoctions ranged from surprisingly simple to incredibly complex.

Today, cakes are just as treasured as they always have been. They're also easier to make than ever. There's no need to resort to a mix. It just won't taste the same as homemade. Besides, with the easy recipes you'll find here, you can expect good results every time.

Cakes made with the special soft wheat flour from White Lily are higher-rising and have visibly more volume than cakes made with other flour brands. You'll be wonderfully pleased with your cake's fluffiness and delicate texture. So will the people who have the honor and pleasure of eating it.

Shortcakes with Fresh Berries and Cream

You'll recognize these recipe instructions from the biscuit chapter. Shortcakes are basically sweet biscuits.

2 cups White Lily Self-Rising Flour

¼ cup sugar

1 large egg

⅓ cup half-and-half

½ cup (1 stick) cold butter

2 to 3 cups sliced strawberries or whole raspberries, sweetened with ¼ cup sugar

1 cup blueberries, optional

1 cup heavy cream, whipped

Preheat oven to 425° F.

Combine flour and sugar. Whisk egg and half-and-half until blended. Divide the butter into pieces and scatter on top of the flour mixture. Work the pieces into the flour with a pastry cutter, two knives, or your fingertips until the pieces are about the size of peas.

Add egg mixture gradually, adding only enough to moisten the flour and hold the dough together. Turn the dough onto a lightly floured surface. Knead gently 2 to 3 strokes.

Using a light touch, pat or roll dough to ½- to ¾-inch thickness. Cut using a floured 2½- to 3-inch biscuit cutter, leaving as little dough between cuts as possible. Gather the remaining dough and re-roll one time. Discard remaining scraps.

Place biscuits 2 to 3 inches apart on ungreased baking sheet. Brush tops lightly with half-and-half or milk. Bake for 12 to 15 minutes, or until golden brown.

Toss berries together. Split shortcakes in half and spoon fruit between layers. Replace top layer and spoon on additional fruit. Add whipped cream on top. Garnish with fresh whole fruit.

Makes 6 to 8 individual shortcakes.

Warm Pecan Shortcakes with Spicy Peach Compote

Shortcakes

2¾ cups White Lily Self-Rising Flour

3 tablespoons sugar

½ teaspoon ground cinnamon

¼ teaspoon ground nutmeg

6 tablespoons cold butter

½ cup finely chopped pecans

1 large egg, lightly beaten

⅔ cup milk

1 cup whipping cream, whipped

Spicy Peach Compote

¾ cup sugar

3 tablespoons cornstarch

¾ cup water

1½ pounds fresh peaches, peeled, pitted, and thinly sliced (3 cups)

1 teaspoon fresh lemon juice

½ teaspoon almond extract

Preheat oven to 450° F.

Combine flour, 3 tablespoons of sugar, cinnamon, and nutmeg.

Divide the butter into pieces and scatter them on top of the flour mixture. Work the pieces into the flour with a pastry cutter, two knives, or your fingertips until the pieces are about the size of peas. Stir in pecans.

Combine egg and milk. Add to dry ingredients gradually, adding only enough to moisten the flour and hold the dough together.

Turn dough out onto lightly floured surface and knead gently 2 to 3 strokes. Roll or pat dough to ½-inch thickness. Cut with 2½- to 3-inch biscuit cutter. Place shortcakes 2 to 3 inches apart on ungreased baking sheet.

Bake for 10 to 12 minutes, or until golden brown.

To make the Spicy Peach Compote, combine sugar and cornstarch in medium saucepan. Add water, stirring until smooth. Stir in peaches. Cook over medium heat, stirring constantly, until thickened and peaches are tender. Remove from heat. Stir in lemon juice and almond extract.

Split the warm shortcakes in half and spoon the peach compote over the bottom halves. Replace shortcake tops and spoon on additional compote. Top with whipped cream.

Makes 6 to 8 individual shortcakes.

Pineapple Upside-Down Cake

Pineapples are an international symbol of hospitality, so this cake is perfect to serve to house guests.

½ cup (1 stick) butter, room temperature, divided

1 cup packed light brown sugar

1 (8½ ounce) can sliced pineapple, drained, or 5 fresh pineapple slices

1 cup granulated sugar

3 large eggs, separated

1 cup White Lily Plain All-Purpose Flour

1 teaspoon baking powder

½ teaspoon salt

½ cup milk

1 teaspoon pure vanilla extract

Preheat oven to 350° F.

In a 10-inch cast iron skillet, melt 4 tablespoons (½ stick) of the butter over medium heat. Sprinkle with brown sugar. Arrange slices of pineapple over brown sugar. Cook until sugar bubbles. Remove from heat.

Cream the remaining 4 tablespoons butter with an electric mixer. Gradually add granulated sugar and mix well. Beat in egg yolks. Combine flour, baking powder, and salt. Combine milk and vanilla. Alternately add milk mixture and flour mixture to egg yolk mixture, beginning and ending with flour mixture. Beat until blended. Whip egg whites until soft peaks form. Fold into batter. Pour batter over pineapple slices in skillet.

Place skillet in oven and bake for 50 to 55 minutes, or until toothpick inserted near center comes out clean. Immediately invert onto heatproof plate. Let skillet remain over cake 5 minutes before removing. Replace any fruit that sticks to skillet.

Makes 6 to 8 servings.

Circa 1930

One, Two, Three, Four Cake
(An Old Recipe)

*This classic recipe from the 1932 White Lily cookbook is named for the amounts of the main
ingredients, making them easy to remember. Even in the 1932 cookbook,
the name included the subtitle — An Old Recipe.*

1 Scant cup butter

2 Scant cups sugar

3 Cups White Lily Flour

4 eggs

1 Cup cold water

2 Teaspoons baking powder

1 Teaspoon flavoring

Cream shortening, add sugar, then eggs, one at a time, beating all the while. Add water and
flour alternately, sift baking powder in last of flour, flavor to taste. Bake in loaf 1 hour very
slowly, or in three layers ½ hour in moderate oven (350°), fill as desired. This is fine foundation for fruit cake.

Light-As-A-Cloud Angel Food Cake with Strawberry Glaze and Sweetened Whipped Cream

Angel food cakes appeared in the original 1900s White Lily cookbook. They are best when fresh strawberries are in season.

1¼ cups White Lily Plain All-Purpose Flour,
  sifted before measuring
1¾ cups sugar, divided
1¾ cups egg whites (12 to 14 eggs)
1½ teaspoons cream of tartar

¼ teaspoon salt
2 teaspoons pure vanilla or almond extract
Fresh strawberries
Strawberry Glaze (recipe follows)
Sweetened Whipped Cream (recipe follows)

Preheat oven to 375° F.

Sift flour and ¾ cup of the sugar three times. Set aside.

Beat egg whites, cream of tartar, and salt until soft peaks form. Gradually add remaining 1 cup sugar. Continue beating until very stiff peaks form.

Sift one-fourth of the flour mixture over egg white mixture and gently fold in. Repeat with remaining flour mixture, one-fourth at a time. Fold in extract. Spoon batter into ungreased 10-inch tube pan. Run knife through batter gently to remove air pockets. Bake in lower third of oven for 35 to 40 minutes, or until cake springs back when lightly pressed with finger.

Cool cake by inverting the tube of the pan over a heat-proof bottle. To remove cake, carefully run a thin knife between the cake and pan. The top will stick to the pan. Again use the knife to loosen.

Serve with fresh strawberries, Strawberry Glaze, and Sweetened Whipped Cream.

Makes one 10-inch cake.

Variation

Chocolate Angel Food Cake: Substitute ¼ cup cocoa powder for ¼ cup of flour.

Strawberry Glaze

1 cup sliced fresh strawberries
½ cup water

⅓ cup sugar
2 teaspoons cornstarch

Bring strawberries and water to a boil in a heavy saucepan over medium-high heat and cook for 2 minutes. Strain berries and juice into small bowl pressing down to release all juice. Discard pulp and seeds. Pour strawberry liquid into saucepan. Add sugar and cornstarch and cook over medium heat until thickened and clear.

Serve by spooning the sauce over the cake or spoon sauce into heavy-duty plastic storage bag, cut corner of bag. Drizzle sauce on plate.

Makes ⅔ cup.

Sweetened Whipped Cream

1 cup whipped heavy cream
2 tablespoons confectioners' sugar

½ teaspoon pure vanilla extract

Whip cream with confectioners' sugar and vanilla until peaks form. Do not whip after peaks stay in place.

WHIPPING EGGS MADE SIMPLE

When whipping egg whites, be sure all bowls and beaters are free from any fat or oil. In addition, make sure that no yolk gets mixed in with the whites. Any kind of fat will keep the whites from whipping properly. Since the egg whites are the secret to good angel food cakes, the amount of whipping is important. Overwhipped egg whites become dry and are no longer smooth. You can "repair" the dried out egg whites by whipping in more whites until the mixture is smooth again. If you use egg yolks in other recipes, stock up the whites in the freezer until you have enough for an angel food cake.

PERFECT INGREDIENTS MAKE PERFECT CAKES

Measuring ingredients correctly is so important. To measure flour, spoon lightly into a measuring cup made for dry ingredients. Level the flour over the top with a spatula (see page 18). To measure other ingredients, be sure to use liquid measuring cups and dry measuring cups as needed. Shortening or brown sugar should be packed into the measuring cup before leveling off.

For all the cakes in this book, unsalted butter is recommended.

Ingredients for making cakes need to be at room temperature. Place eggs in slightly warm tap water for 30 minutes before using. Butter may be softened at room temperature or microwaved on low (20 percent power) for 20 seconds, but be careful not to melt it.

Substitution for buttermilk: Add 1 tablespoon of lemon juice to 1 of cup milk.

PANS AND OVENS

Use light colored baking pans whenever possible. Dark colored pans cause cakes to overbake around the edges.

Grease and flour pans well. Even if you use a nonstick cooking spray, still be sure to lightly dust the pans with flour. The flour coats the fat and helps promote higher rising in the pan.

Be sure your oven is the right temperature. An oven's temperature is often not what it shows on the setting. Check your oven periodically with an oven thermometer. An oven that cooks too hot causes peaked "volcano" type cakes. An oven that cooks too cool makes cakes dry.

The White Lily Cake™

The first White Lily White Cake™ recipe appeared in the 1951 cookbook. We've simplified the longtime favorite a little. Mixing the batter is quick and easy and uses only one bowl. With the addition of frosting, you can transform these white cake layers into gooey caramel cake, luscious strawberry cake, mouthwatering coconut cake, and many more.

2½ cups White Lily Plain All-Purpose Flour

1½ cups sugar

1 teaspoon baking powder

1 teaspoon salt

½ teaspoon baking soda

1 cup buttermilk

¾ cup vegetable shortening

4 egg whites

1 teaspoon pure vanilla extract

1 teaspoon almond, lemon, or coconut extract, or 1 additional teaspoon pure vanilla extract

Preheat oven to 350° F. Grease three 8-inch or two 9-inch round pans or one 13 x 9 x 2-inch pan. Line bottom of pans with waxed paper cut to fit. Grease and flour the waxed paper and flour the edges of pan.

In a mixing bowl, combine flour, sugar, baking powder, salt, and soda. Add buttermilk and shortening and beat two minutes. Add egg whites, vanilla extract, and choice of extract. Beat an additional 2 minutes, scraping sides of bowl as needed. Evenly spread batter into prepared pans. Tap pans on counter several times to remove air bubbles.

Bake for 22 to 25 minutes, or until toothpick inserted near center comes out clean. Cool on wire rack 10 minutes before removing from pans. Finish cooling on wire rack. (The 13 x 9-inch cake may be cooled and frosted in pan, if desired.)

Makes two 9-inch layers, three 8-inch layers, or one 13 x 9 x 2-inch cake, 12 to 18 servings.

Sour Cream Pound Cake with Fresh Fruit and White Chocolate Sauce

2¾ cups White Lily Plain All-Purpose Flour

½ teaspoon salt

¼ teaspoon baking soda

1 cup (2 sticks) unsalted butter, room temperature

3 cups sugar

6 large eggs, room temperature

1 cup sour cream

½ teaspoon lemon extract

½ teaspoon almond extract

½ teaspoon pure vanilla extract

Confectioners' sugar, optional

Fresh pineapple, bananas, berries, or kiwi, sliced or hulled

White Chocolate Sauce (recipe follows)

Preheat oven to 325° F. Grease and flour a 10-inch tube pan or two 8½ x 4½ x 2¾-inch loaf pans.

Combine flour, salt, and baking soda. Set aside. Cream butter in electric mixer on medium speed for 2 minutes, or until light and fluffy. Gradually add sugar and continue to beat 5 to 8 minutes, or until light and fluffy. Add eggs, one at a time, beating 1 minute after each addition. Scrape batter from sides of bowl often.

Add flour mixture to batter alternately with sour cream, beginning and ending with dry ingredients. Stir in by hand or beat on low speed just until each ingredient is combined. Add lemon, almond, and vanilla extracts. Pour batter into pan(s).

Bake for 1 hour and 15 to 30 minutes, or until wooden toothpick inserted in center comes out clean. Cool 15 minutes on wire rack. Remove from pan(s) and cool. Sift confectioners' sugar over cake, if desired. To serve, arrange cake slice and fresh fruit on individual plates and drizzle with White Chocolate Sauce.

Makes one 10-inch cake or two 8-inch loaves, 12 to 16 servings.

Variation

Lemon Pound Cake: Prepare cake as listed above except omit the almond and vanilla extracts and add 1 tablespoon fresh lemon juice and 2 tablespoons freshly grated lemon zest.

White Chocolate Sauce

6 ounces white chocolate, broken in pieces (1½ cups)
½ cup heavy cream
¼ teaspoon almond extract

Combine white chocolate and cream in heavy saucepan. Cook and stir over low heat until chocolate is melted and mixture is blended. Stir in extract. Let cool slightly to thicken.

Spoon cooled sauce into heavy-duty plastic storage bag. Cut corner of bag to drizzle sauce over cake or fruit.

Makes 2 cups.

HOW TO KNOW WHEN THE CAKE IS DONE

Check the oven often as the cooking time nears an end to determine if the cake is done. (Always open and close the oven door gently.) Remove the cake as soon as a toothpick inserted near the center comes out clean, with no batter or crumbs clinging to it. You can also press lightly on the top of the cake to determine doneness. If it springs back, the cake is ready to come out.

Circa 1900

Lane Cake

Found in the oldest White Lily cookbook, this recipe was originally called Prize Cake in an 1898 cookbook by Mrs. Emma Rylander Lane. The Atlanta woman who submitted the recipe to White Lily, Mrs. G. L. Gartner, added raisins and nuts to Mrs. Lane's coconut filling. You may want to frost the sides with ½ recipe for Fluffy Frosting (see page 121).

3 Cups White Lily Flour	1 Cup butter
1 Cup sweet milk	2 Cups sugar
6 Egg whites	3 Teaspoons baking powder
1 Teaspoon vanilla	

Cream butter and sugar, add egg whites unbeaten; mix well; add milk and flour in two portions and beat until free of lumps. Sift in the baking powder with flour; add vanilla and bake in three layers.

Filling for Lane Cake

6 Yolks, 1½ Cups sugar, ½ Cup butter

Put on stove in double boiler and cook until thick; remove from stove and add 1 cup chopped raisins, 1 cup chopped nuts, 1 small coconut, 1 tablespoon vanilla; beat until cool and spread on layers.

Toasted Coconut Cake

The White Lily Cake (see page 115)
Fluffy Frosting (see page 121)
2 cups shredded coconut, divided

Prepare The White Lily Cake in round layers according to instructions. Prepare Fluffy Frosting. Add ¾ cup shredded coconut to frosting. Frost cake.

To toast the remaining 1¼ cups of coconut, preheat oven to 300° F. Sprinkle coconut onto a baking sheet in a single layer. Toast for 8 to 10 minutes, stirring often.

Cool completely. Sprinkle over frosted cake.

THE ICING ON THE CAKE

Cool cake completely before frosting. Brush cakes lightly to remove loose crumbs.

Place wax paper under the edges of the cake to keep the plate clean. Carefully remove the wax paper when you're done icing.

Frost the bottom layer top side down. Trim rounded tops for better stacking. Save one rounded layer for the top, and place it on the top of the cake rounded side up. Frost sides first, then the top of the cake.

Raspberry Almond Torte

The White Lily Cake (see page 115)
White Buttercream Frosting
2 cups raspberry preserves
¾ to 1 cup sliced almonds
1 cup fresh raspberries

Prepare The White Lily Cake in round layers according to instructions. If using two 9-inch layers, split each layer horizontally to make 4 layers. If using three 8-inch layers, do not split. Place one layer on serving plate. Spread with ½ cup raspberry preserves. Sprinkle with ¼ cup almonds. Repeat until the top layer. Spread the top with the remaining raspberry preserves. Frost sides of cake with White Buttercream Frosting. Press remaining almonds into the side of the cake and sprinkle fresh raspberries on cake's top.

White Buttercream Frosting

4 cups (1 pound) confectioners' sugar
¼ cup milk
1 teaspoon pure vanilla extract
¼ teaspoon salt
4 tablespoons unsalted butter, room temperature

Combine confectioners' sugar, milk, vanilla extract, and salt. Add butter and beat until smooth. Add additional milk one teaspoon at a time if needed for spreading consistency.

Red Velvet Cake

Said to have been invented at the Waldorf-Astoria in New York, red velvet cake has become such a favorite in the South that it's now considered a Southern dessert.

2 tablespoons unsweetened cocoa powder

2 ounces red food coloring

½ cup vegetable shortening

1½ cups sugar

2 large eggs

1 teaspoon pure vanilla extract

2¼ cups White Lily Plain All-Purpose Flour

1 teaspoon salt

1 cup buttermilk

1 teaspoon vinegar

1 teaspoon baking soda

Fluffy Frosting or Cream Cheese Frosting (see p. 123)

Preheat oven to 350° F. Grease and flour two 9-inch round pans or three 8-inch round pans. Blend food coloring and cocoa together. Cream shortening and sugar until light and fluffy. Add eggs one at a time, beating well after each addition. Blend in vanilla and cocoa mixture. Combine flour and salt. Add flour mixture alternately with buttermilk, beginning and ending with flour mixture. Stir in vinegar, using a spoon, until well blended. Add soda, gently stirring until well blended.

   Pour into prepared pans. Bake for 25 to 30 minutes. Cool on wire rack 10 minutes before removing from pans. Cool completely on wire rack. If using 9-inch pans, split layers horizontally. Frost with Fluffy Frosting or Cream Cheese Frosting.

Makes two 9-inch layers or three 8-inch layers, about 12 servings.

Fluffy Frosting

The almond extract gives this frosting a unique flavor.

½ cup (1 stick) unsalted butter

½ cup vegetable shortening

1 cup sugar

3 tablespoons White Lily Plain All-Purpose Flour

⅔ cup milk, room temperature

1 teaspoon almond extract or pure vanilla extract

Cream butter, shortening, and sugar until light and fluffy. Add flour 1 tablespoon at a time, mixing well between each addition. Add milk and extract. Beat until light and fluffy.

Makes 3½ cups.

Circa 1920

Blackberry Jam Cake – (Orange Filling)

Jam cake originated in either Tennessee or in nearby Kentucky. This recipe is unique because it uses orange filling rather than frosting. It also omits mixing and baking instructions — certain things were assumed in those days! We baked this cake at 350° F for 30 minutes and determined that "butter size of walnut" is about 2 tablespoons. The list of ingredients tells you to cream the two cups of sugar with the cup of butter and lard, and the "oranges grated" means peel only.

5 Eggs (leave out 3 yolks for filling)	1 Cup raisins
1 Cup butter and lard mixed	1 Cup nuts
2 Cups sugar creamed with shortening	1 Cup jam
1 Teaspoon each of cinnamon, cloves and allspice	4 Cups of flour
1 Teaspoon of soda dissolved in 1 cup of buttermilk	

Filling:

3 Whole oranges grated	Butter size of walnut
2 Cups of sugar	Yolk of 3 eggs

Cook until thick enough to spread when cool.

Delicious - Mrs. Thomas A. Hanserd, Monroe, Ga.

Black Walnut Cream Cake

A Tennessee lady known as Grandma Grace has served this cake made with the native American black walnut at many church dinners-on-the-grounds through the years. It's perfect for special occasions because it has the character of a hard-to-make cake but is really extremely easy. This cake is best when served the same day it is made.

2¼ cups White Lily Self-Rising Flour

1 cup chopped black walnuts

3 large eggs

2 cups sugar

1½ cups heavy cream

½ cup whole milk

2 teaspoons pure vanilla extract

Cream Cheese Frosting

Preheat oven to 350° F. Grease and flour three 8-inch or two 9-inch round pans or a 13x9x2-inch pan.

Blend flour and nuts in small bowl. Set aside.

In a large mixing bowl, beat eggs for 1 minute or until light and fluffy. Add sugar and beat for 30 seconds or until blended.

Combine heavy cream and milk. To egg-sugar mixture, add flour and nuts alternately with milk and cream, beginning and ending with flour-nut mixture. Add vanilla. Beat on medium-high speed for 2 minutes.

Bake for 25 to 30 minutes, or until a toothpick inserted near the center of the cake comes out clean. Cool in pans for 10 minutes on wire racks. Remove from pans and finish cooling on wire racks. Cool completely. Frost with Cream Cheese Frosting. Sprinkle top lightly with additional black walnuts if desired.

Makes two 9-inch layers, three 8-inch layers, or one 13 x 9 x 2-inch cake, 12 to 18 servings.

Cream Cheese Frosting

1 (8 ounce) package cream cheese, room temperature

8 tablespoons (1 stick) unsalted butter, room temperature

3 to 4 cups (1 pound) confectioners' sugar

1 teaspoon pure vanilla extract

Beat cream cheese and butter until smooth. Add confectioners' sugar and vanilla, and beat until smooth. Add more or less confectioners' sugar to obtain desired consistency.

Chocolate Layer Cake with Chocolate Silk Frosting

If you like, use Dutch-process cocoa for a darker, more chocolatey cake.

2 cups White Lily Plain All-Purpose Flour

2 cups sugar

¾ cup unsweetened cocoa powder, sifted

1 teaspoon baking soda

½ teaspoon salt

¾ cup vegetable oil

½ cup buttermilk

2 large eggs

2 teaspoons pure vanilla extract

1 cup boiling water

Chocolate Silk Frosting (recipe follows)

Preheat oven to 350° F. Lightly grease three 8-inch or two 9-inch round pans or a 13 x 9 x 2-inch pan. Line bottom of pan(s) with waxed paper cut to fit. Grease the paper and flour paper and pan sides.

Combine flour, sugar, cocoa, baking soda, and salt. Add oil, buttermilk, eggs, and vanilla. Beat for 2 minutes at medium speed. Stir in boiling water until blended. Batter will be thin.

Pour batter evenly into pans. Bake for 30 to 35 minutes, or until toothpick inserted near the center comes out clean. Cool on wire rack 5 minutes before removing from pans. Finish cooling on wire rack. (The 13 x 9-inch cake may be cooled and frosted in pan, if desired.)

Makes two 9-inch layers, three 8-inch layers, or one 13 x 9 x 2-inch cake, about 12 to 18 servings.

Variation

Triple Chocolate Cake: Frost Chocolate Layer Cake with White Chocolate Frosting (see page 125). Press 2 cups semisweet chocolate chips onto sides of frosted cake.

Chocolate Silk Frosting

1½ sticks unsalted butter, softened

1 cup unsweetened cocoa powder, sifted

5⅓ cups confectioners' sugar

¾ cup heavy cream

2 teaspoons pure vanilla extract

Beat butter. Add cocoa, confectioners' sugar, and cream. Blend in vanilla. Beat until smooth and creamy.

White Chocolate Frosting

4 (2 ounce) squares white chocolate

4 (3 ounce) packages cream cheese, softened

1½ sticks butter, room temperature

1 teaspoon pure vanilla extract

3 cups confectioners' sugar

Melt white chocolate over low heat, stirring constantly, or microwave on medium (50 percent power) for 2 to 4 minutes, stirring 4 times. Cool.

In mixing bowl, beat cream cheese until smooth and gradually add melted white chocolate. Add butter and vanilla, beating well. Gradually add confectioners' sugar and beat until smooth and fluffy.

Circa 1900

Old-Fashioned Pound Cake

You'll find quicker-to-prepare pound cakes in the cookbook, but this one is the original — it contains the one pound of each ingredient for which the cake is named. Beating the batter was very important. It took two hours by hand or only one hour (!) by electric mixer. Baking powder, invented in 1850s, was a fairly recent addition.

1 Pound sifted White Lily Flour (4½ cups)

1 Pound butter (2 cups)

1 Pound sugar (2¼ cups)

1 Pound eggs (10 large)

1 Teaspoon baking powder (optional)

1 Teaspoon vanilla

½ Teaspoon lemon extract

Cream flour and butter together until fluffy and smooth. Add flavorings. Beat eggs until fluffy and lemon colored. Add sugar gradually, beating constantly. Add the egg mixture gradually to the butter and smooth. One teaspoon baking powder may be added, but real old-fashioned pound cakes contained none. If made by hand, beat batter about 2 hours. When an electric beater is used, beat about 1 hour, or until batter looks very light and fluffy. Fill greased, paper-lined loaf pans half full and bake in a slow oven (325° F) for 1½ hours.

Yield: 2 loaves.

Moist and Spicy Carrot Cake with Pineapple

Mace is the outer portion of nutmeg, but has its own distinctive aroma and a milder flavor. You may substitute nutmeg if you don't have mace on hand.

4 eggs

2 cups sugar

1½ cups vegetable oil

2¼ cups White Lily Self-Rising Flour

1 teaspoon ground cinnamon

¼ teaspoon ground cloves

¼ teaspoon ground allspice

¼ teaspoon ground mace or nutmeg

2 cups finely grated carrots

1 (8¼ ounce) can crushed pineapple with juice

1½ cups chopped pecans, divided

Cream Cheese Frosting (see page 123)

Preheat oven to 325° F. Grease and flour two 9-inch cake pans or three 8-inch cake pans.

Beat eggs in large mixing bowl until light and fluffy. Add sugar and oil. Stir in flour and spices.

Add carrots, undrained pineapple, and ¾ cup of the pecans.

Bake for 30 to 35 minutes, or until toothpick inserted near the center comes out clean. Cool in pan for 10 minutes. Remove from pans and finish cooling on wire racks. Cool completely. Frost with Cream Cheese Frosting. For garnish press remaining pecans on sides of cake.

Makes two 9-inch layers or three 8-inch layers, about 12 servings.

STORING CAKES

Cakes can usually be stored for three days in an airtight container at room temperature.

Freezing works well for most cakes. If the cake is frosted, freeze it before wrapping. Wrap tightly with plastic wrap first, then cover with a layer of aluminum foil To thaw an unfrosted cake, leave wrapped and let defrost at room temperature for four to five hours. To thaw a frosted cake, unwrap and defrost overnight in the refrigerator. Bring to room temperature before serving.

Appalachian Apple Stack Cake

This cake is a tradition at weddings in the Appalachian regions of the South. Each guest brought one "stack," or layer, to the celebration. The more popular the bride and groom, the higher the cake.

5¼ cups White Lily Plain All-Purpose Flour

1 teaspoon baking soda

1 teaspoon baking powder

1 teaspoon salt

1 teaspoon ground cinnamon

2½ packed cups brown sugar

1 cup vegetable shortening

2 large eggs

2 teaspoons pure vanilla extract

½ cup buttermilk

Apple Filling

Confectioners' sugar, optional

Preheat oven to 425° F. Grease and flour 9-inch cake pans. Reuse pans as needed.

Combine flour, soda, baking powder, salt, and cinnamon. Set aside. Cream brown sugar and shortening 2 to 3 minutes. Then beat in eggs and vanilla.

On low speed, beat in flour mixture alternately with buttermilk, beginning and ending with flour, until just combined. Divide dough into seven (¾ cup) portions.

Bake 10 minutes or until golden brown. Remove from pan and cool completely on wire rack. Stack with hot Apple Filling between layers. Cake is best if you can let it stand 24 hours before serving. If desired, sift confectioners' sugar over top of cake before serving.

Makes seven 9-inch layers, about 16 servings.

Apple Filling

5 cups water

1 pound dried apples

2 cups packed brown sugar

2 teaspoons ground cinnamon

1 teaspoon ground nutmeg

½ teaspoon ground cloves

¼ teaspoon salt

Bring water to a boil in a Dutch oven. Chop dried apples, using a food processor if you have one. Add apples to water. Cook uncovered over medium heat until all water is absorbed, 20 to 25 minutes. Add sugar, cinnamon, nutmeg, cloves, and salt. Simmer 15 minutes, stirring frequently.

Circa 1960

Wacky Cake

This cake was popular in the 1960s as busy people began looking for easy recipes. It's not elegant, but it is good. We don't know why it tells us to wash our hands. We usually assume our readers know this important aspect of cooking!

Wash your hands clean
Take out all ingredients
1½ cups White Lily Plain Flour
1 cup sugar
1 tsp. baking soda
½ tsp. salt

3 tbsp. cocoa
⅓ cup cooking oil
1 tbsp. vinegar
1 tsp. vanilla
1 cup cold water

Mix dry ingredients in 9 x 9-inch pan. Make three holes; pour oil, vinegar, and vanilla in separate holes. Pour water over all. Mix well with fork. Do not beat. Bake at 350° F for 30 minutes. Leave in pan and frost while still warm.

Wacky Cake Topping

½ cup sugar
½ cup milk
¼ stick margarine

1½ tbsp. WHITE LILY Flour
½ cup coconut or chopped nuts

Combine all ingredients and cook until thick. Add ½ tsp. vanilla. Spread on warm cake; top with nuts if desired.

Cookies

The sweet, warm smell of freshly baked cookies brings out the child in all of us. One bite of a crunchy pecan tassie or crisp chocolate chip cookie calls up long-buried memories of coming home from school to a plate of our favorites.

As one of their first sweet treats, children quickly learn to love and appreciate cookies. Every child knows that Santa depends on a plate of cookies and milk at each stop to help him get his great sack of gifts delivered on time. But the truth is that cookies tempt all comers – young and old alike. It's with a wail of woe that the last unlucky person comes up empty-handed from the cookie jar.

The charm of cookies is that they come in all shapes, sizes, and flavors. With such a multitude to choose from, everyone is guaranteed that at least one cookie will tickle their taste buds. Plus, there's practically no better choice than a cookie to satisfy a snack attack or a sweet craving.

The Dutch deserve the credit for introducing cookies to the American culinary scene. In fact, the word cookie comes from the Dutch term "koekje," meaning little cake. However, the cookie goes back much further than that. It is actually thought to date from seventh-century Persia, which was one of the first countries in the world to cultivate sugar.

Of course, everyone knows that it takes at least a little bit of sugar to make a really satisfying cookie. Sugar used to be a hard ingredient to handle – literally. In colonial times, sugar was sold in cones. Cutting it off the cone required a special tool. It was so hard it took an auger, a tool typically used to bore holes in wood, to loosen it. Then it had to be ground in a special sugar mill.

As much as Americans would like to take credit for inventing, introducing, or improving the incredibly edible cookie, they really can't. That's just the way the cookie crumbles.

Chocolate Chip Cookies

Remember coming home from school to a wonderful smell, peeking in the cookie jar, and finding America's favorite variety?

3 cups White Lily Plain All-Purpose Flour

1 teaspoon baking soda

½ teaspoon salt

½ pound (2 sticks) butter, room temperature

1 cup brown sugar, packed

½ cup granulated sugar

2 large eggs, lightly beaten

2 teaspoons pure vanilla extract

2 cups semisweet chocolate chips

1 cup chopped nuts, optional

Preheat oven to 375° F. Very lightly grease baking sheet.

Combine flour, baking soda, and salt. Set aside.

In mixing bowl, cream butter, brown sugar, and granulated sugar. Beat in eggs and vanilla until light and fluffy. Blend in flour mixture. Stir in chocolate chips and, if desired, chopped nuts. Drop by heaping teaspoonfuls onto prepared baking sheet. Bake for 8 to 10 minutes. Cool on wire rack.

Makes 4 dozen cookies.

Note: You can refrigerate the dough for up to 2 days. Increase the baking time by 2 to 3 minutes.

Variation

Chocolate Candy Cookies: Replace the chocolate chips with chocolate chunks, candy coated pieces, or cut-up candy bars.

132

Gourmet Double Chocolate Cookies

Reminiscent of fudge, these cookies are made by pouring a glossy chocolate stream of melted semisweet morsels into the batter. The ultimate touch — hunks of creamy white chocolate and whole macadamia nuts. Unforgettable!

2 cups (12-ounce package) semisweet chocolate chips

8 tablespoons (1 stick) butter, room temperature

¾ cup White Lily Plain All-Purpose Flour

1 teaspoon salt

½ teaspoon baking powder

1 cup sugar

3 large eggs

1 teaspoon pure vanilla extract

2 (6 ounce) packages white chocolate bars, chopped into ¼- to ½-inch chunks

1½ cups (7-ounce jar) lightly salted or unsalted macadamia nuts, whole or coarsely chopped

---

Preheat oven to 350° F. Line baking sheet with aluminum foil shiny side up and grease lightly with non-stick cooking spray.

In a saucepan or in the microwave, melt chocolate chips and butter, stirring often. Allow to cool. Stir flour, salt, and baking powder together. Set aside.

In a mixing bowl, beat sugar, eggs, and vanilla at high speed for 2 minutes. Mix in cooled, melted chocolate and butter on low speed. Add dry ingredients and mix on low speed just until blended. Stir in white chocolate chunks and macadamia nuts.

Drop by heaping tablespoonfuls onto prepared baking sheet. Bake for 12 minutes, or until edges of cookies are set. Reverse the baking sheet front to back once during baking. Cookies will be dry on outside but soft on inside. Do not overbake. Cool 15 minutes on wire rack before removing cookies from foil.

Makes 3 dozen cookies.

Circa 1900

Caramel Cookies

*This simple recipe was recommended for bridge luncheons in the
1900s White Lily cookbook for "fine baking."*

2 cups brown sugar

3 cups White Lily Flour

2 Eggs

½ cup shortening

1 teaspoon soda

1½ teaspoons cream of tartar

Sift sugar free from lumps, sift flour, cream of tartar and soda, add the sugar, cut in the fat
with spatula like pastry, slowly add the well beaten eggs. Place on board and knead well.
Mold into two loaves, place on ice to chill [you can use the refrigerator] or let stand over
night. Cut in thin slices, place on oiled baking sheet. Bake in oven 400° F 10 minutes.

Pecan Shortbread

8 tablespoons (1 stick) butter, room temperature

¼ packed cup brown sugar

1¼ White Lily Plain All-Purpose Flour

½ cup finely chopped pecans

Confectioners' sugar, optional

Preheat oven to 325° F.

With an electric mixer, cream butter and brown sugar for 3 minutes. Stir in flour and pecans by hand just until blended. Shape into ball.

Roll on lightly floured surface to ½-inch thickness. Cut with 1½-inch cookie cutters in whatever shapes you desire. Transfer to ungreased baking sheet. Bake at 325° F for 20 to 25 minutes or until edges are browned.

Cool on wire rack. Sift confectioners' sugar over tops, if desired.

Makes 2 dozen cookies.

KEEPING COOKIES

Cool cookies completely before stacking so they do not stick together or become soggy.

Store soft and crisp cookies separately. Otherwise, crisp cookies will become soft and mushy.

If cookies are fragile, stack with wax paper between layers.

Restore freshness and crispness to cookies by reheating at 300° F for three to five minutes.

Place cookies to be frozen in a single layer in the freezer. Once frozen, stack the cookies between layers of wax paper and pack in freezer wrap or bags. Most cookies freeze well.

Apple Butter Thumbprint Cookies

These cookies were a favorite in the 1950s edition of the White Lily cookbook. We updated the recipe by using apple butter rather than jam.

½ pound (2 sticks) butter, room temperature

½ cup confectioners' sugar

¼ teaspoon salt

1 tablespoon pure vanilla extract

2 cups White Lily Plain All-Purpose Flour

1 cup finely chopped pecans

1 cup apple butter

With an electric mixer, cream butter and sugar. Add salt and vanilla. Stir in flour and pecans until just blended.

Divide dough in half, wrap each half in plastic wrap, and chill several hours or overnight.
Preheat oven to 350° F.

Shape dough into 60 one-inch balls. Place on lightly greased baking sheet. Press thumb gently in the center of each ball to make an indention.

Fill with apple butter. Bake for 15 minutes, or until the edges are lightly browned. Cool on a wire rack.

Makes 5 dozen cookies.

Variations

Peach Butter Thumbprint Cookies: Replace the apple butter filling with peach butter.

Pumpkin Butter Thumbprint Cookies: Replace the apple butter filling with pumpkin butter.

Circa 1900

Gingersnaps

2¾ cups White Lily Flour

2 teaspoons baking soda

1 teaspoon each cinnamon and ginger

¼ teaspoon cloves

1 cup packed brown sugar

¾ cup butter or margarine, softened

1 egg

¼ cup light molasses

Preheat oven to 375° F and lightly grease baking sheets. Combine flour, soda, cinnamon, ginger, and cloves; set aside. Cream sugar and butter or margarine. Beat in egg and molasses until light and fluffy. Stir in flour mixture just until blended. Chill thoroughly.

Shape dough into ¾-inch balls and roll in granulated sugar. Place on baking sheet 2 inches apart. Flatten with bottom of glass dipped in sugar. Bake 8 to 10 minutes or until cookies are set. Cool on wire rack.

Makes 8 dozen.

Double Chocolate Fudge Brownies

This brownie recipe is the hands-down winner from the White Lily Test Kitchen. We love it topped with ice cream.

2 cups sugar

1¼ cup White Lily Plain All-Purpose Flour

½ teaspoon baking soda

½ teaspoon salt

¾ cup unsweetened cocoa powder

½ pound (2 sticks) butter, melted

4 large eggs

2 teaspoons pure vanilla extract

1½ cups (10-ounce bag) semisweet chocolate chips

1 cup chopped nuts, optional

Preheat oven to 350° F. Grease and flour 9 x 13 x 2-inch pan.

Combine sugar, flour, baking soda, salt, and cocoa. Set aside. Mix melted butter, eggs, and vanilla until smooth. Add to flour mixture and stir until moistened. Fold in chocolate chips and, if desired, nuts, and spread batter into pan.

Bake for 35 to 40 minutes, or until toothpick inserted one-inch from center comes out barely moist. Do not overbake. Cool and cut into squares.

Makes 2 dozen brownies.

Variations

Peanut Butter Crunch Brownies: Prepare brownie batter according to instructions. Do not add the chopped nuts. Spread brownie batter in pan. Melt 1½ cups (10-ounce bag) peanut butter chips in a double boiler or in microwave on medium (50 percent power). Stir in 1½ cups chopped peanuts. Swirl peanut butter mixture into brownie batter. Bake as instructed.

Easy Brownie Pizza: This variation is the kid's favorite with its popular pizza shape, colorful candy pieces, and drizzled chocolate. For a super-easy dessert, use White Lily Chewy Fudge Brownie Mix rather than the brownie recipe. Add ½ cup candy coated chocolate pieces to the brownie batter, and bake in a 12-inch pizza pan. Immediately after removing from oven, press additional candy pieces on top of brownie. Melt 1 cup white chocolate chips or peanut butter chips in microwave on medium (50 percent power) for about 30 seconds. Stir and spoon into a plastic sandwich bag. Cut corner of bag and drizzle over the pizza. Makes about 16 servings.

SMART COOKIES

Room temperature ingredients are best for cookies. For best results, use unsalted butter instead of margarine.

Try using a food processor to mix your cookies. Each step takes only a few seconds.

Use a heavy flat baking sheet for cooking. Aluminum baking sheets with shiny surfaces or baking sheets with insulated bottoms provide the best results. Dark baking pans cause cookies to brown too rapidly on the bottom.

Use a light spray of nonstick vegetable oil or grease pan lightly with shortening. It is not necessary to regrease the pan between batches.

Place cookies at least one inch apart unless otherwise instructed.

Cookies generally bake quickly, so watch and time the cooking carefully to prevent overbaking.

Remove cookies from pan and place on racks to cool.

Be sure baking sheets cool to room temperature between uses so that cookies retain their shape.

Circa 1960

Snowballs

The White Lily Baking Primer (For Blooming Good Baking) was published with this recipe. These cookies are also known as Mexican Wedding Cookies, but Snowballs is the best description.

2¼ cups White Lily Flour

¼ teaspoon salt

1 cup butter

½ cup sifted confectioners' sugar

1 cup finely chopped nuts

Sift flour and salt together.

Mix butter, vanilla, and sugar thoroughly. Blend in flour mixture. Mix in nuts. Chill dough.

Heat oven to 400° F.

With hands, roll dough in 1-inch balls. Place on ungreased baking sheet about ½ inch apart. Bake 10 to 12 minutes or until set but not brown.

While still warm, roll in confectioners' sugar. Cool. Roll in sugar again.

Makes about 4 dozen cookies.

Rich Peanut Butter Bars

This chewy treat is White Lily's most requested cookie recipe. It first appeared on bags more than twenty years ago.

½ cup peanut butter

8 tablespoons (1 stick) butter

1½ cups sugar

2 large eggs

1 teaspoon pure vanilla extract

1 cup White Lily Self-Rising Flour

Preheat oven to 350° F. Grease and flour a 9 x 13 x 2-inch pan.

Melt peanut butter and butter in a double boiler, or melt in a microwave on medium (50 percent power) for approximately 2 minutes.

Add remaining ingredients. Stir until blended.

Bake for 25 to 30 minutes, or until a toothpick inserted in the center comes out barely moist. Cool and cut into squares.

Makes 2 dozen bar cookies.

THE BEST BAR COOKIES

Bar cookies and brownies look better when cut straight down. Line baking pan with foil, shiny side down, so that foil comes up over the ends of the pan. Grease and flour the foil. After brownies or bar cookies have cooled, lift the foil and remove from pan. Now the cookies are ready to be cut with a top to bottom motion rather than slicing across the dough. You can also cut creative shapes rather than squares by using cookie cutters such as stars, hearts, or whatever suits your fancy or the season.

Lemon Bars

2½ cups White Lily Plain All-Purpose Flour, divided
½ pound (2 sticks) butter or margarine, softened
½ cup confectioners' sugar, plus additional for sifting on top
2 cups sugar
½ cup lemon juice
4 large eggs
Grated zest of 1 lemon, optional

Preheat oven to 350° F. Lightly grease a 9 x 13 x 2-inch pan.

In a large mixing bowl, combine 2¼ cups of the flour, the butter or margarine, and the confectioners' sugar. Mix until a soft dough forms. Press dough into baking pan. Bake for 20 to 25 minutes, or until lightly browned. Remove from oven.

Meanwhile, beat sugar, lemon juice, the remaining ¼ cup flour, eggs, and lemon zest until well combined. Pour over hot crust. Return to oven and bake an additional 20 minutes, or until set. Cool on wire rack and cut into bars. Sift confectioners' sugar over tops.

Makes about 3 dozen 1½ x 2-inch bars.

Cheddar Cheese Straws

Cookies are supposed to be sweet, but this tangy, tasty snack is a traditional favorite at Southern teas and weddings. If you have a cookie press, you can make these straws into fancy, ridged shapes. But other quick and easy shaping methods are provided here, too.

1½ cups White Lily Plain All-Purpose Flour

¼ teaspoon cayenne pepper

2 cups shredded cheddar cheese, room temperature

8 tablespoons (1 stick) butter, softened

Preheat oven to 375° F. Combine flour and cayenne pepper and set aside.

In food processor or with an electric mixer, combine cheese and butter until smooth. Add the flour mixture.

Make straws using a cookie press with a star attachment, or roll the dough to ⅛-inch thickness and cut into 1 x 2-inch strips.

Bake for 8 to 10 minutes, or until lightly browned.

Makes 8 dozen straws.

Variation

Cheddar Cheese Crackers: Shape the prepared dough into cylinders 2 inches in diameter. Refrigerate for one hour. Slice into ⅛-inch-thick circles. Makes 4 dozen cheese crackers.

Circa 1960

Oatmeal Cookies

1½ cups raisins

1 cup water

2½ cups WHITE LILY FLOUR

½ teaspoon baking powder

1 teaspoon soda

1 teaspoon salt

1 teaspoon cinnamon

¼ teaspoon cloves

¾ cup shortening

½ cup chopped nuts

1½ cups sugar

2 eggs

1 teaspoon vanilla

2 cups rolled oats

Simmer raisins and water in saucepan over low heat until raisins are plump, 20 to 30 minutes. Drain raisin liquid into measuring cup. Add enough water to make ½ cup.

Heat oven to 400° F.

Stir together flour, baking powder, soda, salt, and spices.

Mix shortening, sugar, eggs, and vanilla. Stir in raisin liquid. Blend in flour mixture. Add rolled oats, nuts, raisins.

Drop rounded teaspoonfuls of dough 2 inches apart on ungreased baking sheet. Bake 8 to 10 minutes or until lightly browned.

Makes 7 dozen.

Pecan Tassies

These little tarts are one of the South's favorite finger foods at showers for brides and moms-to-be.

1 (3 ounce) package cream cheese, room temperature

8 tablespoons (1 stick) butter, room temperature

1 cup White Lily Plain All-Purpose Flour

1 cup chopped pecans

1 large egg

¾ packed cup brown sugar

1 tablespoon butter, room temperature

1 teaspoon pure vanilla extract

⅛ teaspoon salt

With an electric mixer, blend cream cheese and butter. Stir in flour until just blended. Form dough into a ball. Wrap with plastic wrap. Chill for 1 hour.

Preheat oven to 325° F.

Shape dough into 24 one-inch balls. Press into ungreased 1½-inch mini-muffin cups or tart pans. Make a shallow shell with the dough. Sprinkle half of the pecans into dough shells.

Beat egg, brown sugar, butter, vanilla, and salt. Pour mixture evenly into dough shells. Sprinkle tops with remaining pecans.

Bake 20 to 25 minutes, or until crust is lightly browned and filling is set. Cool in pans on wire rack.

Makes 2 dozen cookies.

Pies, Puddings, and Cobblers

In the old days, young women baked pies to be auctioned at church socials. The young men would bid on the "pie" that caught their eye. The winning bidder not only won the pie, but the opportunity to share a slice with the young woman who baked it. Although pie-making skills are no longer a criterion for dating and marriage, the pie is as highly regarded as ever. In fact, we love pie so much, we've worked it into our popular vocabulary. It's not uncommon to hear people call loved ones by any number of sweet names, including "sugar pie," "honey pie," "cutie pie" and "sweetie pie."

If you want to cook up the perfect dessert to please your "sweetie pie," you simply can't go wrong with a pie, especially one with a flaky, tender, homemade crust. Of course, the pie you make will depend on your preferences and the season. A piping hot, fresh fruit pie topped with a dollop of vanilla ice cream is dreamy in the summer, while pecan and pumpkin pies are fall favorites and Thanksgiving traditions. Creamy buttermilk pie is a delight for all seasons.

Although the filling is essential, the key to pie perfection is in the crust. Your first crust will taste delicious, but practice does come in handy. As with any art, the perfect-tasting, perfect-looking pie crust may take a few tries to master. However, it's well worth the effort.

For cobblers, there's no need to fuss with the crust. With plenty of flavors to choose from, they make delightful desserts for friends and family. In Georgia, these quick and easy desserts used to be called "cut and come again" pies. And with good reason. It's the rare person who can eat just one piece.

Once you know the secrets of pastry dough, say goodbye to store-bought, premade pie crusts. With White Lily at your side and a little practice and patience, you too can make perfect home-made pie crusts — crusts your friends, neighbors, and special "honey pie" will rave on and on about, long after they've forgotten what was in the filling.

Old-Fashioned Apple Pie

This apple pie recipe is the "American pie." It has been published in a century of White Lily cookbooks.

1 double-crust recipe from Flaky Pie Crust (see page 150)

6 to 9 medium Granny Smith or Golden Delicious apples, peeled, cored, and sliced (6 to 7 cups)

1 tablespoon fresh lemon juice

¾ cup sugar

3 tablespoons White Lily Plain All-Purpose Flour

½ teaspoon ground cinnamon

⅛ teaspoon ground cloves

⅛ teaspoon ground allspice

4 tablespoons cold butter

1 large egg, lightly beaten

1 tablespoon sugar

Preheat oven to 425° F.

Prepare pie dough for double-crust pie. Place bottom crust in 9-inch pan and chill.

Toss apple slices with lemon juice in large bowl. Mix sugar, flour, cinnamon, cloves, and allspice. Add mixture to apple slices and toss.

Fill the bottom crust with the apple mixture, mounding it carefully. Dot the mixture with small pieces of cold butter.

Place the prepared top crust over the apples. Brush with the beaten egg, and sprinkle with sugar.

Bake for 45 to 50 minutes. Cover rim lightly with aluminum foil if the crust is browning too much. Cool on wire rack. Serve warm or at room temperature.

Makes 8 servings.

Variations

Gingered Pear Pie: Substitute Bartlett pears for the apples and replace spices with 1 teaspoon cinnamon and ¼ teaspoon each ginger, nutmeg, cardamom and salt.

Cinnamon Apple Pie: Increase sugar to 1 cup and cinnamon to 1 tablespoon.

Flaky Pie Crust

This pie crust is the easiest and best crust for sweet or savory dishes. It is tender and flaky. For the most color and flavor, use milk and butter-flavored shortening. For a lighter color and more mellow flavor, use ice water and plain shortening.

For Single-Crust Pie

1½ cups White Lily Plain All-Purpose Flour

½ teaspoon salt

½ cup plain or butter-flavored shortening

3 to 4 tablespoons ice-cold water or milk

For Double-Crust Pie

2 cups White Lily Plain All-Purpose Flour

½ teaspoon salt

⅔ cup plain or butter-flavored shortening

4 to 5 tablespoons ice-cold water or milk

In a medium bowl, combine flour and salt. Work in shortening with a pastry cutter, two knives, or your fingertips until mixture resembles coarse crumbs.

Sprinkle one tablespoon ice-cold water or milk over part of mixture. Toss gently with fork and push to side of bowl. Repeat just until the mixture is moistened and you can form it into a ball. The dough should hold together when picked up and pressed and should not crack.

Flatten ball of dough into disks (one disk for one crust, two disks for double-crust). Wrap tightly with plastic wrap and refrigerate dough for 30 minutes to overnight.

Remove one disk of dough from the refrigerator. Turn pastry out onto very lightly floured surface. If the dough is too hard, allow it to sit for 5 minutes to soften. Roll the dough gently. Use a back and forth motion from center. Do not roll over the edge or it will be thin. Turn the dough 45 degrees between each roll to keep it round. If dough sticks to the surface, dust surface lightly with flour. Roll to 12 inches in diameter for a 9-inch pie.

Transfer dough into a 9-inch, 4-cup capacity pie plate, being careful to avoid stretching pastry. Trim edge of the pastry ½ to ¾ inch beyond the edge of the pie plate.

For single-crust pies, fold the extra pastry under to build up the edge. Flute the edge of the pastry by using the forefinger of one hand and pinching the dough next to it between your forefinger and thumb of the other hand. Continue around pie.

At this point, cover and refrigerate the pie crust for 30 minutes to overnight before baking unless otherwise specified in recipe.

Two of the favorite methods for preparing a top crust are:

Solid Top: Roll crust as described above. Cut around the edge so it is even and 10 inches in diameter. Transfer the crust over the filling, being careful not to stretch the pastry. Tuck the edge of the crust under the bottom crust and press to seal. Flute the edge of the pastry as described above. Cut several slashes in the top to allow steam to escape. Brush with a lightly beaten egg and sprinkle with 1 tablespoon sugar. Use a decorative design with the slashes if you wish. You can also decorate the top with cutout pieces of the leftover crust.

Lattice Top: Roll dough as described above, then cut into strips ½ inch in width. Some strips should be 9 inches long. (A pizza cutter works well for this.) Place strips over pie in a horizontal direction. Fold alternate strips back and place a strip vertically across top. Unfold strips, and fold the strips back that are under the last vertical strip. Place another strip vertically across. Continue until pie is completed. Tuck the strip edges under the bottom crust and press to seal. Flute the edge of the pastry as described above. Brush the dough with a lightly beaten egg, being careful not to get egg on filling.

Circa 1900

Never Failing Pie Crust

This recipe appeared in the first White Lily cookbook, and was so popular it was reprinted in almost every edition. The boiling water used here makes this a tender, rather than a flaky, crust. The recipe was contributed by Mrs. W. L. Adkins from Atlanta, Georgia.

1 Cup lard
⅔ Cup boiling water
3 Cups flour
1 Teaspoon salt
1 Teaspoon baking powder

Put lard into bowl and pour over it the boiling water. Measure flour, salt, and baking powder into sifter and sift into bowl of hot water and melted lard. Stir with a spoon until a stiff dough is made. Set away to cool. Never use while hot. Will keep a week if kept in a cool place.

Southern Pecan Pie

Pecans were the nuts of the New World, and settlers depended on them for sustenance. Now we depend on them for one of our richest desserts. But to make it even richer, add chocolate chips for a treat that originated in Kentucky.

1 single-crust recipe from Flaky Pie Crust (see page 150)

3 large eggs

1 cup light corn syrup

⅔ packed cup brown sugar

4 tablespoons butter, melted

⅛ teaspoon salt

½ cup chopped pecans

1 cup pecan halves

Whipped cream

Preheat oven to 425° F.

Prepare dough for single-crust pie. Place crust in 9-inch pan and chill.

Beat eggs in large bowl. Beat in corn syrup, brown sugar, butter, and salt. Mix well. Stir in chopped pecans and pour into unbaked pie shell. Arrange pecan halves evenly over the top.

Bake for 15 minutes. Reduce temperature to 350° F and continue baking for 30 to 35 minutes or until knife inserted slightly off center comes out clean. Cool on wire rack. Serve with whipped cream.

Makes 8 servings.

Variation

Chocolate Pecan Pie: Reduce corn syrup to ½ cup and omit the brown sugar. Add 1 cup chocolate chips to the filling mixture when adding pecans. Top with pecan halves and an additional ½ cup chocolate chips.

Buttermilk Pie

Buttermilk is what remains after making butter. Most buttermilk on the market is skim milk.

1 single-crust recipe from Flaky Pie Crust (see page 150)

¼ cup White Lily Plain All-Purpose Flour

1¾ cups sugar

½ teaspoon salt

8 tablespoons (1 stick) butter, softened

3 large eggs, slightly beaten

½ cup buttermilk

1½ teaspoons pure vanilla extract

1 teaspoon ground nutmeg

Fresh berries or fresh sliced peaches

Preheat oven to 400° F.

Prepare dough for single-crust pie. Place crust in a 9-inch (2-inch deep) pan and chill.

Combine flour, sugar, and salt in large mixing bowl. In smaller bowl, combine butter, eggs, and buttermilk. Add egg mixture to flour mixture. Stir in vanilla.

Pour into chilled unbaked pie crust. Sprinkle top with nutmeg.

Bake for 45 to 50 minutes. Cool on wire rack. Place pie in refrigerator to store. Serve with fruit.

Makes 8 servings.

Pumpkin Pie

Pumpkin pie was eaten by the pilgrims at Thanksgiving and has been a tradition ever since. Although you may use fresh pumpkin, most are happy with the results from canned. And it's much easier!

1 single-crust recipe from Flaky Pie Crust (see page 150)

3 large eggs

1 (16 ounce) can solid pack pumpkin (not pumpkin pie filling)

¾ cup sugar

½ teaspoon salt

1 teaspoon ground cinnamon

½ teaspoon ground ginger

¼ teaspoon ground nutmeg

⅛ teaspoon ground cloves

1½ cups half-and-half

Whipped cream

Preheat oven to 425° F.

Prepare dough for single-crust pie. Place crust in 9-inch pan and chill.

Beat eggs in large bowl. Add pumpkin and mix well. Add sugar and salt and thoroughly combine. Add cinnamon, ginger, nutmeg, and cloves. Stir in half-and-half. Pour carefully into unbaked pie shell.

Bake for 15 minutes at 425° F. Reduce temperature to 375° F and bake 35 to 40 minutes, or until knife inserted one inch off center comes out almost clean. The center of the pie should be soft and shake slightly. Cool on wire rack. Serve with whipped cream. Place in refrigerator to store.

Makes 8 servings.

Variation

Sweet Potato Pie: **Replace pumpkin with 1½ cups mashed sweet potatoes. In place of sugar, use ¾ cup packed brown sugar.**

Circa 1930

Rhubarb Pie

Green rhubarb tastes about the same, but the pink-colored vegetable makes a prettier pie.

½ recipe Standard Pastry
3½ cups cut-up pink rhubarb
1 cup sugar

3 tablespoons White Lily Flour
1 egg
Whipping cream

Prepare pastry. Roll out bottom crust. Fit into pan. Spread rhubarb evenly over pastry. Combine sugar and flour. Sprinkle on rhubarb. Beat egg. Pour in measuring cup and fill to 1 cup level with whipping cream. Pour egg and cream on rhubarb. Bake in moderately hot oven (400° F.) 10 minutes. Reduce heat to moderate (350° F.) and continue baking about 50 minutes, or until rhubarb is tender.

Yield: One 8-inch pie.

Peaches and Cream Pie with Raspberries

Choose peaches by the aroma. The "peachier" they smell, the better they taste.

1 single-crust recipe from Flaky Pie Crust (see page 150)

⅔ cup sugar

¼ cup cornstarch

¼ teaspoon salt

1½ cups milk

2 large egg yolks, lightly beaten

1 tablespoon butter

½ teaspoon pure vanilla extract

¼ teaspoon almond extract

2 cups sliced fresh ripe peaches, divided

¾ cup peach preserves

2 teaspoons unflavored gelatin

2 tablespoons cold water

½ cup fresh raspberries

Preheat oven to 450° F.

Roll out dough for single-crust pie and place in pie plate. Prick bottom and sides of pastry with a fork to prevent crust from shrinking. Line crust with foil and fill with dry beans, rice, or pie weights. Bake for 10 to 12 minutes or until lightly browned. Cool completely.

Combine sugar, cornstarch, and salt in small saucepan. Gradually add milk, mixing well. Cook over medium-high heat for 5 minutes or until thickened, stirring constantly.

To keep eggs from scrambling, stir a small amount of hot mixture into egg yolks. Return egg yolk mixture to hot mixture. Continue cooking for 2 minutes, stirring constantly. Remove from heat. Stir in butter, vanilla extract, and almond extract. Cool.

Arrange 1 cup sliced peaches in cooled, baked pastry shell. Spoon cream filling over peaches. Refrigerate.

Heat preserves in small saucepan. Strain preserves to make peach glaze. In small bowl, soften gelatin in 2 tablespoons cold water. Add gelatin to ½ cup of the hot glaze, stirring until gelatin dissolves. Cool until mixture is the consistency of unbeaten egg whites.

Arrange the remaining peaches and the raspberries over pie filling. Pour or spoon glaze evenly over peaches and raspberries. Chill 4 to 6 hours, or until firm.

Makes 8 servings.

Chocolate–Peanut Butter Cream Pie with Chocolate Crust

Grown mostly in Georgia, Alabama, and Florida, peanuts show up in many Southern desserts.

Chocolate Crust

1 cup White Lily Plain All-Purpose Flour

¼ cup firmly packed brown sugar

2 tablespoons unsweetened cocoa powder

½ teaspoon salt

⅓ cup shortening

2 to 3 tablespoons ice water

Chocolate–Peanut Butter Filling

2 tablespoons White Lily Plain All-Purpose Flour

⅔ cup sugar

1 tablespoon cornstarch

¼ teaspoon salt

2½ cups milk

3 large egg yolks, lightly beaten

1 cup creamy peanut butter

1 teaspoon pure vanilla extract

½ cup semisweet baking chocolate cut in small pieces

½ cup heavy cream

2 tablespoons confectioners' sugar

¼ cup dry-roasted peanuts, chopped

Preheat oven to 450° F.

To make the crust, combine flour, brown sugar, cocoa, and salt. Work shortening into flour mixture with a pastry cutter, two knives, or your fingertips until mixture resembles coarse crumbs. Add water one tablespoon at a time. Toss with fork. Repeat just until the mixture is moistened and you can form it into a ball. The dough should hold together when picked up and pressed and should not crack. Flatten ball and chill 30 minutes.

Roll dough out on lightly floured surface to a 12-inch-diameter circle. Place in 9-inch pie plate. Trim excess pastry from edges. Fold edges under, and flute as described in Flaky Pie Crust recipe (see page 150). Prick bottom and sides with fork. Bake for 8 to 10 minutes or until lightly browned. Cool.

To make the filling, combine the flour, sugar, cornstarch, and salt in a heavy saucepan. Gradually stir in milk. Cook over medium heat, stirring constantly, for 5 minutes, or until thickened. Gradually stir about one-fourth of hot mixture into beaten egg yolks. Add the egg yolk mixture back into saucepan and cook, stirring constantly, until mixture thickens. Stir in peanut butter and vanilla until melted. Remove from heat.

Stir chocolate pieces into mixture, leaving some chunks unmelted. Pour hot mixture into baked Chocolate Crust. Let stand for 1 minute, then swirl melted chocolate chunks using knife. Cool completely.

Whip heavy cream and confectioners' sugar until it forms soft peaks. Spread whipped cream over the top of pie and garnish with chopped peanuts. Place pie in refrigerator to store.

Makes 8 servings.

Lemon-Blueberry Tart with Spice Crust

Spice Crust

1½ cups White Lily Plain All-Purpose Flour

2 tablespoons sugar

¾ teaspoon salt

¼ teaspoon ground ginger

⅛ teaspoon ground mace or nutmeg

8 tablespoons (1 stick) cold butter

1 large egg yolk, lightly beaten

3 to 4 tablespoons ice-cold water

Lemon-Blueberry Filling

2 tablespoons grated fresh lemon peel

⅔ cup fresh lemon juice

1 cup sugar

8 tablespoons (1 stick) butter

2 eggs, lightly beaten

½ cup heavy cream, plus additional heavy cream for whipped topping

1¾ cups fresh blueberries

Preheat oven to 375° F.

To make the Spice Crust, combine flour, sugar, salt, ginger, and mace or nutmeg in medium bowl. Cut in butter with a pastry cutter, two knives, or your fingertips until mixture resembles coarse crumbs. Add egg yolk and water, tossing lightly with fork until mixture is evenly moistened and holds together. Shape mixture into a ball. Wrap with plastic wrap and refrigerate 30 minutes.

Press pastry onto bottom and sides of a 9-inch fluted tart pan, or divide pastry and press into six to eight 3-inch tart pans. Prick bottom of crust with a fork. Bake for 12 to 15 minutes, or until lightly browned. Cool.

To make the Lemon-Blueberry Filling, combine lemon peel, lemon juice, sugar, and butter in 1½ quart microwave-safe container. Microwave on high (100 percent power) 2 to 3 minutes until butter melts. Stir. To keep eggs from scrambling, gradually stir ¼ cup of hot mixture into eggs. Return egg mixture to hot mixture, stirring constantly. Microwave on medium high (70 percent power) 3 to 4 minutes, or until thickened. Stir after 2 minutes. Cool.

Whip ½ cup of the heavy cream until soft peaks form. Fold into lemon mixture. Spoon into pastry. Chill 4 hours, or until firm.

Whip additional heavy cream. Before serving, arrange blueberries on top and garnish with whipped cream.

Makes one 9-inch tart, or six to eight individual tarts.

160

Circa 1960

Jiffy Apple Crisp

Also known as Brown Betty, apple crisp has been a quick and easy favorite for decades.

4 to 5 apples, peeled, cored and sliced thin

1 cup **WHITE LILY** Self-rising Flour

¾ cup sugar

1 egg, beaten

5⅓ tablespoons (⅓ cup) butter, melted

½ tsp. Nutmeg

Place apples in baking dish. Combine flour, sugar, and egg. Spread over apples and drizzle with butter; sprinkle with nutmeg. Bake at 350° for 30 to 40 minutes. Serve with cream or ice cream if desired.

Persimmon Pudding

Persimmons are a Southern autumn fruit that have been used to make everything from beer to a substitute for coffee. They are bitter until they are fully ripe, so make sure you use very soft fruit with wrinkled skin. Persimmons freeze well and will ripen while thawing. This pudding is a Thanksgiving tradition in some Southeastern homes.

1 quart fresh persimmons

3 large eggs, lightly beaten

1¼ cups sugar

1½ cups White Lily Plain All-Purpose Flour

1 teaspoon baking powder

1 teaspoon soda

½ teaspoon salt

8 tablespoons (1 stick) butter, melted

2 teaspoons ground cinnamon

1 teaspoon ground ginger

½ teaspoon ground nutmeg

1 cup raisins, optional

1 cup pecans, optional

Preheat oven to 325° F.

Over a large bowl, press persimmons through a colander to remove skin. Makes approximately 2 cups of persimmon pulp.

Stir in the remaining ingredients.

Pour mixture into a 9 x 13-inch baking pan. Bake for 1 hour, or until firm. Serve warm, topped with whipped cream.

Makes 12 servings.

Peach Cobbler with Biscuit Topping

Peaches from Georgia and South Carolina have become a cobbler favorite. Choose peaches with a sweet aroma. Green peaches have been harvested too soon and will not ripen.

Peach Filling

10 to 12 medium fresh peaches, peeled, pitted,
  and sliced (6 cups), or 2 (16 ounce) packages
  frozen peach slices, thawed
1 cup sugar
2 tablespoons White Lily Self-Rising Flour
½ teaspoon ground cinnamon
2 tablespoons butter

Biscuit Topping

1⅔ cups White Lily Self-Rising Flour
¼ cup sugar
4 tablespoons cold butter
⅓ to ½ cup milk
1 tablespoon melted butter
1 tablespoon sugar

Preheat oven to 450° F.

To make Peach Filling, combine peach slices, sugar, flour, and cinnamon in a large saucepan. Heat on medium high for 5 minutes, or until mixture is hot and sauce begins to thicken.

Melt butter in 9 x 9-inch or 11 x 7-inch baking pan. Pour peach mixture into melted butter. Set aside.

To make Biscuit Topping, combine flour and sugar. Cut in cold butter with a pastry cutter, two knives, or your fingertips until mixture resembles coarse crumbs. Add the milk gradually, stirring in only enough to moisten the flour and hold the dough together. Turn dough onto lightly floured surface. Fold the dough in half and press lightly 2 or 3 times so that it can be rolled and will not stick. Roll dough out to about ¼ inch thick and cut with a 2-inch biscuit cutter. Press biscuits gently on top of peach mixture. Drizzle with melted butter and sprinkle with sugar.

Bake for 15 to 20 minutes, or until biscuits are golden brown. Serve warm, and for a special touch, top with ice cream.

Makes 6 to 8 servings.

Variations

Blueberry Cobbler: For filling, replace the peaches with 4 cups fresh blueberries or 2 (16 ounce) packages frozen blueberries, reduce the sugar to ¾ cup, and replace cinnamon with 1 teaspoon fresh lemon juice.

Blackberry Cobbler: For filling, replace the peaches with 4 cups fresh blackberries or 2 (16 ounce) packages frozen blackberries, and replace cinnamon with 1 teaspoon grated orange rind.

Index